Amazing Cakes

Amazing Cakes

Recipes for the World's Most Unusual, Creative, and Customizable Cakes

Instructables.com

Edited and Introduced by

Sarah James

Skyhorse Publishing

Skyhorse Publishing books may be purchased in bulk at special discounts for sales promotion, corporate gifts, fund-raising, or educational purposes. Special editions can also be created to specifications. For details, contact the Special Sales Department, Skyhorse Publishing, 307 West 36th Street, 11th Floor, New York, NY 10018 or info@ skyhorsepublishing.com.

Skyhorse® and Skyhorse Publishing® are registered trademarks of Skyhorse Publishing, Inc.®, a Delaware corporation.

www.skyhorsepublishing.com

10 9 8 7 6 5 4 3 2 1

Library of Congress Cataloging-in-Publication Data is available on file.

ISBN: 978-1-62087-690-9

Printed in China

Disclaimer:
This book is intended to offer general guidance. It is sold with the understanding that every effort was made to provide the most current and accurate information. However, errors and omissions are still possible. Any use or misuse of the information contained herein is solely the responsibility of the user, and the author and publisher make no warrantees or claims as to the truth or validity of the information. The author and publisher shall have neither liability nor responsibility to any person or entity with respect to any loss or damage caused, or alleged to have been caused, directly or indirectly, by the information contained in this book. Furthermore, this book is not intended to give professional dietary, technical, or medical advice. Please refer to and follow any local laws when using any of the information contained herein, and act responsibly and safely at all times.

Table of Contents

Introduction

If you're looking to take your cake to the next to the next level with unusual shapes, alternating interior colors, surprise contents, or fun themes, you've come to the right place. These amazing cakes were created by members of the Instructables community, innovative amateurs tired of boring old sheet cakes or, God forbid, store-bought cakes.

These recipes contain step-by-step directions written by the very bakers themselves. The pictures you see are not doctored cake glamor shots. Nor are they fondant monstrosities made to look better than they taste. Instead, each cake was made with a purpose:

to delight someone they love with a cake that looks and tastes good. The techniques and tools they use are all pretty ordinary, but the authors created something extraordinary with them.

Clearly this is not a comprehensive collection of all the wonderful cakes ever created. The hope is that you'll be inspired to combine ideas to create the cake that you envision. This is just a starting point. It is up to you to adapt, modify, improve, and ultimately bake a cake that makes you and your loved ones happy.

DotatDabbled says it best in the introduction to her Dragon Cake, "You don't have to be a professional to attempt something this cool!"

All the projects in this book were first featured on Instructables.com. Instructables is the most popular project-sharing community on the Internet. We provide easy publishing tools to enable passionate, creative people like you to share their most innovative projects, recipes, skills, and ideas.

Instructables has more than 100,000 projects covering all subjects, including crafts, art, electronics, kids, home improvement, pets, outdoors, reuse, bikes, cars, robotics, food, decorating, woodworking, costuming, games, and more. Check it out today!

* Special thanks to Instructables Interactive Designer Gary Lu for the Instructables Robot illustrations!

Section 1
Animals

Monkey Brain Cake

By Linda Vandermeer
(BubbleandSweet)
(http://www.instructables.com/
id/Monkey-Brain-Cake/)

Eeeek! Chilled monkey brains anyone? Well, if the brains are Jell-O and they are served with a slice of chocolate cake, maybe you won't pass up this treat—made famous in the movies but made slightly more appetizing in this Instructable. This would make an awesome Halloween dessert and would be an especially gruesome table centerpiece.

The preparation for this cake is best spread over three days:
- Day 1: bake the cake and make the ganache
- Day 2: remaining Steps 1 through 7
- Day 3: just prior to serving Step 8

The whole cake does take a bit of work, but if you like you can omit some steps, which will not only save time but will also reduce the equipment and ingredients required, making the cake a little bit more economical. If you like, you can omit the hand painting and just add some extra black fondant in the nostrils. Also, the addition of the Persian fairy floss in Step 8 is completely optional. Or you can just skip straight to Step 7 and make up some brains to serve with raspberry sauce for an easy yet scrumptiously scary treat.

Ingredients and Equipment

- 2 chocolate cakes (mine were chocolate mud and 8" × 3.25")
- Cake board (approx 8")
- Ganache (chocolate and cream)
- White ready-rolled fondant or Pettince, 20 oz or 600 grams[1]
- Black ready-rolled fondant or Pettince, 50 grams or 1.75 oz (or color your own from the white using black gel food color)[2]
- Black, white, and ivory gel food color
- Tylose powder
- Small brush
- Edible glaze, black dusting powder, and large brush
- Large rolling pin
- Small sharp knife
- Small fondant rolling pin

---

[1]Ready-roll fondant, gel food color, cake decorating tools, tylose powder, and d[...] powder available from cake specialty stores, hobby and craft stores (e.g., Micha[...] Spotlight (Australia)), or eBay.
[2]Fondant dries out really quickly—keep it in an airtight container or Zip-loc bag [...] use and work fast.

- Cake decorating flower/leaf tool
- Cake smoothers (kind of optional)
- Brain mold[3]
- 2 packs jelly crystals (I used raspberry and grape)
- Evaporated low-fat milk (carnation non fat)
- Powdered gelatin
- Oil spray
- Raspberry sauce (or strawberry)
- Optional white Persian fairy floss and scissors[4]

Note: I placed a piece of parchment paper between the cake and the cake board so I could slip the carved cake directly onto the cake stand prior to Step 4. This was purely for my presentation. Do not do this if you are serving directly from the cake board, as the parchment paper makes the cake slide around.

Step 1: Stack the Cake

To make ganache, heat 400 grams of cream until boiling and add to 800 grams of finely chopped milk chocolate. Allow to rest for a couple of minutes and then whisk until smooth. Allow the ganache to set at room temperature overnight.

Cut the tops off each cake to make them even, and then cut each cake in half so you have four even cakes. Place one cake slice on top of a cake board, add a good dollop of ganache, and spread it around evenly. Place another layer of cake on top, then more ganache, then other layer of cake. Repeat until you [hav]e four layers of cake with a layer of [ganac]he between each layer. Cover with [a layer] of plastic wrap, place it in the [fridge a]nd chill until firm.

[my] Jelly Mold on eBay.
[f]loss is available from good delis or specialty food purveyors.

Step 2: Carve the Cake

Remove the cake from the fridge. Using a knife, carve the cake into shape. See the pictures for examples of how the carved cake should look. You will need to carve off the front sides to make a skull-type shape, tapering in towards the bottom. Then, about ¾" needs to come off the front (the top layer) for the eye/eyebrow area. Do not discard the pieces you carve off, reserve them for use in Step 3.

Cover the carved cake with a layer of ganache and make as smooth as possible. If necessary, you may need to do this in more than one stage by covering the cake in ganache, smoothing it with a hot knife or spatula, and then repeating the process. Make the ganache on the top of the cake as smooth and flat as possible. Y'know, for resting brains on later.

Step 3: Add the Face Detail

Take the reserved off-cuts of the cake and add enough extra ganache to make a smooth truffle mixture by crumbing the cake through your fingertips and mixing the ganache in. I just use my hands to squish it together. You might need to heat the ganache in the microwave for a few seconds if you are finding it difficult to mix. Remember, the off-cuts already have some ganache, so crumble the cake first and add the ganache slowly until you have achieved your desired truffle consistency.

The finished truffle should hold together well, hold shape, and not be too sloppy. Take one piece of truffle, around a couple of teaspoons, and press onto the front of the cake to make a nose. Using your fingertips, shape into a nose with nostrils. Take another larger truffle piece and press into the front of the cake to make an oval-shaped mouth protruding from the bottom center of the cake. See the picture for guidance. Cover the mouth and nose detail with a thin layer of ganache. Roll another couple of pieces of truffle mixture and make shapes that are half circles, around the size of half a ping pong ball. These truffles will be the eyes. Any leftover truffle mixture can be frozen for later use or made into cake pops.

Note: The nose in the pictures is a different shape from the finished cake. I was working from memory and checked a picture at a later stage. Luckily, the truffle mixture is very easy to rework.

Step 4: Make the Mouth Detail

Knead the black fondant until pliable. Place a small amount of vegetable fat on your workbench and roll out the fondant with a small plastic rolling pin. Cut out a shape to cover the mouth section of the cake.

Use some of the remaining black fondant to cover the half circles of truffle "eyes" you made in Step 3. Reserve 2 tablespoons of white fondant. Knead the remaining white fondant until smooth and add in a little black to make the fondant gray and some tylose powder to make the fondant stronger. Knead until the color is well distributed and even.

Take a couple of tablespoons of the gray fondant and roll it out with a small rolling pin until it is quite thin at one side, with a thicker rim around ⅖" wide

(the lip) and around 3.25" long. Wrap it around the front bottom of the cake to make a bottom lip. Push it into place under the chin area and, using a sharp knife, trim off any excess. Use the cake decorating tool to mark indents along the lip area to look like creases in the skin.

Take the reserved white fondant, shape small uneven ovals, and press them onto the mouth area just above the lip. If you like, use a tool to mark decay lines in the teeth.

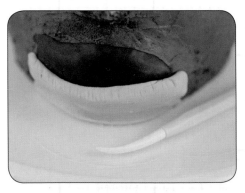

Step 5: Cover the Cake with Fondant

Measure around the outside of your cake, and then measure the height of your cake. Add another ½" to each measurement: that will be the size fondant rectangle you will need. Dust the workbench with a little corn flour (corn starch) and, using a large rolling pin, roll out the fondant until it is quite thin. It should be a long rectangle that is at least as long and wide as your measurements. Use a sharp knife (or pizza cutter) to cut the rectangle to the required size.

In the middle section of the fondant at the bottom, cut out a half circle that will be the open mouth area, around 2.36" at the biggest and tapering down to be 4.72" wide.

Working quickly, wrap the gray fondant around the cake and join it together at the back, trimming off any overhang where the fondant joins. There should be around ⅗" overhang around the top of the cake, which is where the brain will sit. It will act as a dam to hold the brain and raspberry sauce.

I placed some foil in a couple of spots to hold up the fondant while it dried. Press the fondant into the eye socket areas and around the mouth, leaving enough black showing for the teeth to be inserted later. Make sure that the fondant covers the bottom of the cake evenly and that no ganache is showing. Press around the nose area, using the cake decorating tool to press in the nostrils until you are happy with the shape. Add an indent in the middle of the nose with the back of the cake tool. The truffle mixture underneath should have a little give at this stage, so you can still move it around a little to get your desired shape.

Mix a small amount of the gray fondant with a little water to make a thick paste. Place a little paste onto the eye area and press in the eyes. If they are a little big, quickly remove them and trim until you are happy with the size.

Roll out a small amount of fondant as thin as possible to make eyelids. Cut to shape and press onto the eyes, covering the top half. Using a cake tool, smooth the edges as much as possible in the corners to make the join look as seamless as possible. Don't stress too much about the top; it will be covered with the eyebrows.

Take another piece of fondant and shape it into a long log. Use a little more of the fondant mixed with water to "glue" this log into place. Use the cake decorating tool to shape the log into an eyebrow. I made an indent on each side just above the nose and then used the sharp side of the tool to make long shallow strokes in the fondant to look like hair. Place a food safe item between the eye and brow to hold in place while it dries (I used some folded foil).

Make more long shallow hair indents in the fondant around the cheek area. Then, use the same technique with shorter strokes to give the lips texture. Using a brush, paint on a very sheer small amount of white food color to the lip, upper cheek (under the eyes), and middle brow area. Allow to dry for a while until the fondant is firm to touch.

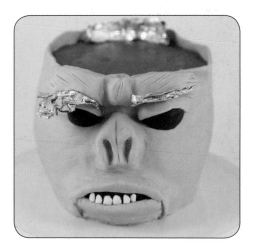

Step 6: Hand Paint Face Details (Optional)

Paint on some edible glaze to the eyes to make them shiny. I mixed my glaze with some black food color to give it a deep look. Use another brush to paint in the nostrils and the eyelid area with black food color. Take a very thin (00) brush and carefully paint in the long shallow indents you have made around the eyebrow area. Take a large full brush and add black dusting powder to the cheek areas, similar to the way you would apply makeup blush. I added some black dusting powder around the eye areas and nose center as well. Mix a very small amount of ivory color with white and paint around the teeth to give a decayed look. Roll out a very thin rope of grey fondant. Add to the very edge of the eyelid where it meets the eye. If mud cake and ganache have been used, the cake can be made to this stage up to three days before serving, stored in a cardboard box at room temperature. Do not store in an airtight container or in the fridge.

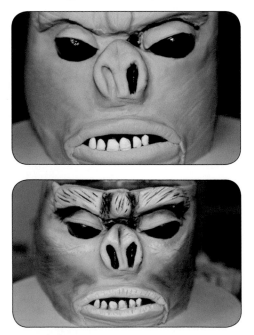

Step 7: Make the Jelly Brain

I made the jelly very firm so it would hold during slicing. If you prefer, you can omit the extra gelatin and/or add more liquid for a wobblier version. Pour two packets of jelly (I used one grape and one raspberry) into a large bowl with 3 teaspoons of powdered gelatin. Add 1 cup of boiling water and mix well until all the crystals are dissolved. Add 1 cup of evaporated low fat milk and mix gently until combined.

Spray the brain mold with a little oil and pour the jelly into the mold. I checked on the cake to see how large the brain cavity would be and only filled the mold up to that spot, which was around half filled. I didn't quite use all the jelly mixture. Pop in the fridge until required. It is best to make the jelly the night before serving to ensure it will be set for the final step.

edge of the eyebrows and cheek area. Separate the fairy floss as much as possible, cut to length with scissors, and gently press onto the edible glue. Serve immediately.

Bubble and Sweet

Step 8: Insert Brain, Add Sauce, and Serve

To serve, unmold the jelly and place in the "brain" cavity of the cake. Pour a little raspberry sauce over the top of the brain.

If you will be adding fairy floss hair, work quickly to brush on a small amount of edible glue (make glue by mixing a little tylose powder with water) to the

For my child's fourth birthday, he wanted a dragon party. So I decided to make him a cake with a dragon on it. This was a *really* impressive cake that, although time consuming, was not that difficult to do.

Note: I am not a professional baker, and I'm sure there are things I've gotten "wrong," but that's one reason I did this Instructable—to show that you don't have to be a professional to attempt something this cool! You can see the original cake in the pictures (the dragon laying on top of the cake) and then a mini version I made with the leftovers to document how it was done. This technique could be used to make a full-size dragon cake or a dragon mold placed on top of an iced cake as I did. Of course, you don't have to make a dragon . . . there are lots of things that could be made with this technique. And remember, you can always cheat and buy a store-bought cake, then make the littler dragon version to go on top of it!

Not including time to make the fondant or the cake mixture, the mini dragon that I did just for this tutorial took about forty-five minutes. For a time reference, the big dragon cake took me all day basically, but that included baking all the cakes, plus cupcakes, plus making the icing . . . and I'd never done anything like this before! From a cost perspective, this is really pretty inexpensive. No expensive ingredients (lots of cake mix, powdered sugar, and so forth), just the cost of your time!

So how's it *taste*? Really yummy! The marshmallow fondant used for the dragon tastes much better than regular fondant to me. And the cake inside the dragon is rich and thick. Everything is edible. The dragon is of my own design, based on my illustration, but I was inspired to put it on top of a cake by a cake I saw on Flickr.

Step 1: Materials/Ingredients
For Base Cake
- Two-layer cake, from mix, prepared as directed on box
- Cream cheese icing. (Of course, if you're in a hurry, a plain cake pre-iced from the store will also work.)

For Dragon

- 1 layer of cake—about half of a box from a typical quality cake mix, like Duncan Hines. (I used the rest of the second box for cupcakes. I had some left over, so one layer was more than enough. I made the mini-dragon, shown throughout this tutorial, from what I had left over.)
- Approximately 1 to 2 cups of cream cheese icing
- Marshmallow fondant (one batch is more than enough and can be made well in advance). The recipe is found at http://whatscookingamerica.net/PegW/Fondant.htm and is really easy to do; it requires only a few simple ingredients, and the resulting fondant is tasty and easy to work with. You could, of course, use store-bought fondant or another recipe, but this worked for me.
- Food coloring (I used a gel) to color the fondant
- Pastel candy corns (available around Easter) or similar candy for horns and claws
- Corn starch
- Silicon mat or parchment paper
- Rolling pin
- Thin cardboard or paper or Styrofoam plate
- Toothpicks
- White modeling chocolate or ten pieces of soft, moldable candy, like light-colored tootsie rolls or starburst. (For the original dragon, I made the modeling chocolate and half of the recipe found at http://www.joyofbaking.com/ModelingChoc.html, and I prepared the steps associated with it in advance. It was not difficult, but for the mini-dragon, I just used tootsie rolls, which worked almost as well for much less work—though I doubt it's as tasty!)

Decorations

- Malted milk eggs
- Pastel candy corns
- Whatever you like!

Cream Cheese Icing

My recipe is easy and yummy. For this project (cake, plus extra cupcakes), I made a double batch. For a single batch, you need:

- 1 stick butter, softened
- 1 package of cream cheese (lower fat is fine, but not nonfat), softened
- 1 pound powdered sugar (aka: confectioners, icing sugar)

Beat butter and cream cheese until smooth in your mixer. Slowly add powdered sugar on lowest speed. Then, beat on medium until the mixture is smooth and creamy. Or you can just pick up three or more store bought jars I guess; you don't have to use cream cheese icing per se, but that's what worked for me.

Step 2: Prepare your Cakes

In my example, I use red-velvet cake for the dragon and white for the base cake. I would actually recommend using a lighter colored cake for the dragon, in retrospect.

Dragon Cake

Crumble up one layer of cake into a large bowl. Spoon in several large spoonfuls of icing. Continue mixing until icing is incorporated. Add additional icing as necessary. You're looking for a soft, moldable consistency that sticks together. If you've ever made cake balls, this is similar. You should be able to gently press your cake mixture into ball form and it stick together.

Base Cake

If you've made your own base cake, ice the two-layer cake with the cream cheese frosting.

Step 3: Building the "Skull"

Since fondant does not hold shapes very well, I decided to build a base shape for the head and just cover it with fondant. For my original cake, I used modeling chocolate, which I modeled into an approximate head shape in advance and stuck in the refrigerator, ready to go (see ingredients for instructions). For the mini-dragon, I "cheated" and used pastel tootsie rolls (kneaded together into a ball) to build a stiff "skull" and it seemed to work almost as well. Note: I used orange, but any light color will do, as it will be covered completely. Whatever material you use, shape to your approximate head shape. Think of a skull—leave indentations where you want the eyes to be and bumps up for the nostrils. If it's a little soft, refrigerate to make it easier to work with.

This can be done ahead of time and refrigerated, which I recommend. Note: I'm not sure this is really necessary (you could probably skip this and use a technique similar to the next steps with cake under the fondant), but I found it to be the easiest way to get a nicely shaped head.

Step 4: Laying Out and Constructing the Dragon

Mark a sheet of parchment paper with a circle about the size of the top of your cake. You'll use this to lay out the dragon prior to placement on the cake. Take a paper plate or cardboard and cut out a shape the approximate size you want the body section of the dragon to be. This will be used as a temporary base to hold your dragon body while you're covering it with the icing/fondant. Lay it out on your circle to ensure it fits nicely. You can place your head in the circle as well and note where you'd like the tail to go.

Now the fun part! Take a good-sized handful of the cake and pack it lightly into an oblong ball, using your base shape as a guide Note: Pictured here is the size of the smaller mini-dragon.

Step 5: Preparing the "Skin"

The outside of the dragon is pretty much all rolled fondant. For mine, I prepared the fondant (and even colored it) well in advance, just to save on added stress at the last minute. If you're starting with white fondant, you'll need to color it. I prepared about half as orange (with red/yellow food coloring gel), then a third of the remainder as blue, a third as green, and the rest as white, just in case! (You only need a little white for this design.) Wear gloves or be prepared to get your fingers dyed a bit as you knead the color into the fondant by hand. This will take a little while, but the fondant must be kneaded prior to rolling anyway.

Note: For all of this step, refer to the marshmallow fondant recipe directions previously referred to if you need more info. They have good tips and I found the instructions easy to follow.

Start with your base color (in my case, orange). On parchment paper or a silicone mat, take a ball of the kneaded

13

orange fondant (rub with corn starch to avoid sticking) and roll to about ¼" thick. Your fondant should be in an oblong shape, large enough to drape over your body section with several inches to spare. Note: The pictures are from the smaller dragon; the larger dragon requires a larger circle.

on top of an upturned cup or something else that will hold it up in the air. You'll be using gravity to help you get a nice drape. Drape the fondant circle over your cake ball and smooth. Lift the body and turn it over. Remove the base. Tuck the sides of the body under (but leave where the neck and tail should go untucked). See the photos. Place it back on your layout circle. Note: Photos are of the small dragon.

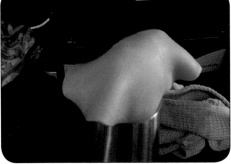

Step 6: Covering the Body

You have two options here. You can ice the body with cream cheese icing prior to this step, or you can skip it. On the original, I did ice the body, but it was difficult, and though it may have added some smoothness (and did cover up my too dark cake), I'm not sure it was worth the effort. For the second mini dragon, pictured here, I skipped the cream cheese icing and I think it looks about as good. Place your cake body (on its base)

Step 7: Cover the Head

Since you already have your skull shape, the head is easy. With a small circle of rolled fondant, drape over the head and wrap under, trimming the excess. Leave where the head will connect with the neck untucked for now. Press lightly so any details and ridges from your skull are visible. Lay it back out on your circle with the body and plan your neck and tail. Note: Photo shows small dragon.

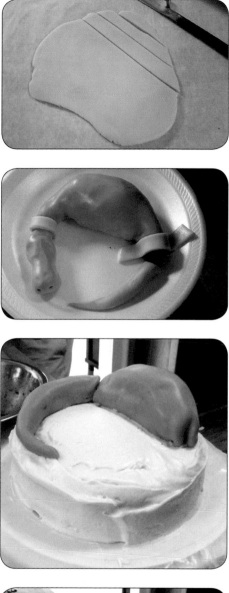

Step 8: Build the Neck and Tail

Now, figure out what you'll need for the neck and the tail. For the larger dragon, I repeated Steps 4–6 to make a neck and tail that was filled with cake. For the smaller dragon, I just shaped some of the excess fondant from the body and head into a neck and added a rolled-up piece of fondant for the tail. The places where they join will be covered in strips of a different color, so the joints don't have to be super neat. See the pictures for more info. Then, cut strips of your other fondant colors, and cover the joints. Drape over, trim off the excess, and tuck the ends under. Note: Save the scraps from the strips, you can use them in the decorating later. Also note that the smaller dragon could be worked with on a plate and then transferred to the cake. I built the larger one on the actual cake, which was a little more difficult, but I didn't want to mess it up in transferring it. If you build yours on the cake, don't worry too much about messing up your base icing—you will a bit—we'll clean it up at the end.

Step 9: Face and Eyes

Eyes (see pictures)
- Ball of white fondant
- Smaller ball of colored fondant (green in example)
- Small balls of skin-colored fondant (orange here)

Place green ball in the center of the white ball and press them together. Flatten the orange fondant, as shown, with your fingers. Press it onto the top of the ball. This is the eyelid and will show partially when you place it on the head. You can play around with the placement of the eyelid and eyeball for different looks. If you cover part of the green with the orange lid, he'll look sleepier. Press the balls into the two eye indentations in the head.

Mouth

Use a toothpick to carefully press in a line for the mouth (see pictures). Use a straw to press in the curved cheek line.

Nostrils

Use the end of a chopstick or something similarly rounded to press in where the nostrils should be.

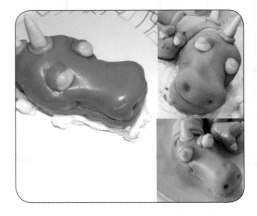

Step 10: Add Arm and Leg

You're now in the decorating stage, and you can do this stuff in any order you like. I think it's probably best to put your arm and leg on first, though you'll note in the pictures I had already done some decorating that will be covered in the next step. The arm and leg are somewhat trial and error. Don't worry if they look a little funny, they can always be somewhat obscured by the eggs. Also, you may want to place your dragon on the cake to do this, if you haven't already. Cut off the tips of six or so candy corns, as they make nice claws!

Leg

Make a small cake ball and wrap it with fondant. Place it on the dragon's side, next to tail. Model fondant into an approximate foot shape (basically a flat triangle, with toes). Insert claws into the toes. Tuck the foot under your leg ball.

Arm

Model fondant into a cylinder for the arm. Split into two or three "fingers" and add claws to the end (see picture). Stick the end to the body close to the neck. If you want to, you could place the claws of the hand on a malted milk egg! It gives extra dimension and covers up flaws with the hand.

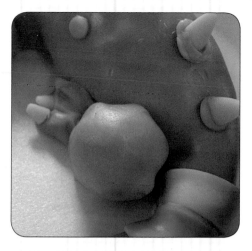

ball of fondant to the cut end and stick it onto your dragon. I did the head and down the back, but be creative! Note: If it's going to be a few days before you serve this, you may want to hold off on placing the spikes until the day of serving. I noticed the candy corn got a little soft, maybe because it got too warm.

Spots

Using a large straw (like a big one from McDonalds) or something else circular, cut out circles and then stick them to the sides of the dragon wherever you like. I used a melon baller to cut out larger circles on the larger dragon.

Step 11: Add Spikes, Spots, and Wings!

Spikes

Cut the ends off more candy corns. (I found they didn't stick well if you tried to leave them whole.) Attach a scrap

Wing (3D)

Cut an approximate wing shape (see pictures for the general shape) out of rolled fondant. Attach a toothpick as shown in the picture. Smooth the wing's

17

shape as necessary. Press the toothpick through the "skin" of the back at an angle, so the wing sticks up. (For the back side of the dragon, I just stuck on the wing so it hung down the back of the cake, with no 3D effect.)

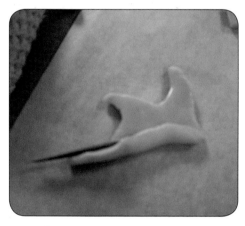

Step 12: Final Decorating Steps

If your dragon is not yet on your cake, you need to carefully transfer it over there. If he is on your cake, you probably need to clean up your icing a bit. I used a piping bag (or a plastic bag with a hole cut in the corner) to pipe icing around the edge of the cake and the dragon to hide any sins or areas where I had disturbed the base icing during decorating. If you're going for the dragon egg look, place malted milk eggs in the center. I also did a ring of pastel candy corns around the bottom for a spiky look. But use your imagination! Cover and place in a cool room, but do not refrigerate (fondant doesn't look good after refrigeration). I hope you enjoyed this tutorial and that it has inspired you to go create something cool of your own! I also did cupcakes to go with this (it was a big party!) with extra malted milk "dragon eggs" on top.

Two 9" round cakes, frosting, decorations, and an unquenchable thirst for adventure are all you need.

Step 1: The Raw Materials

- Two 9" round cakes. Cakes made from scratch will be denser and stronger than a cake mix, but you love the Duncan Hines, don't you? Just be forewarned that the time you save using a mix will be spent cursing during the frosting crumb coat.
- Two batches of frosting. We did a butter cream with 50/50 butter/ vegetable shortening. Dye one batch green. Keep half of the second batch white and dye half blue.
- Rolled fondant. We don't know what this stuff is, but we were darn sure we weren't going to make it. Found some multi-colored fondant at Michael's, a big box craft store. Buy the nonstick mini rolling pin while you are at it.

- Cinnamon red hot candies for the eyes
- Candy corn for the tail spikes
- Chocolate chips for toenails
- Toasted coconut for the prehistoric grass
- One cardboard cake board, half-sheet size
- Frosting pipe tips and bags. Use a star tip. Yes, this makes a difference, so don't skimp here. Really.
- A partner. Not required, but could speed things up during frosting or at least help pass the time.

Step 2: The Body

Bake the cakes and cool completely. Take them out of the pan and find the center of one cake. Cut the cake in half with a bread knife. Put the two halves together with cuts edges aligned and place on a work surface as pictured.

Step 3: The Appendages

Ever heard the advice, "measure twice, cut once?" Unless you are a black belt, Paleolithic pastry chef who can think in three dimensions of cake, you will probably want to make a paper template to design the head, legs, and tail. I drew the template in the picture, and you generally will want to cut the paper in the same shapes I used. Cut a 9" circle of paper and lay it on top of the second cake. Draw the tail and head in one half and the legs in the other. Cut out the paper pieces and arrange them on your body segment to see how they look. Tweak and repeat as necessary. When you are feeling lucky, carve 'em and stack 'em. Oh, and you may want to fix the head to the body with some toothpicks. Just in case the birthday party gets a little rowdy. Move all pieces to the cake board. Use white frosting to join the body halves together, then join the appendages to the body. Trim the corners and square edges off the feet and shoulders if you like.

Step 4: The Skin

Roll the fondant out ⅛" thick. Hand cut the fondant with a small knife into some diamond shapes for the plates on the dinosaur's back. Detail the plates with a toothpick to give them a ribbed texture. Spread a thin layer of green frosting over the cake. This is called the crumb coat—and for good reason, as much of the crumbs pull away and get mixed up in the frosting. Use a very light hand on the cut surfaces of cake. Did you use a cake mix instead of making one from scratch? Are you cursing now? Tip: Crumb coat one half. Have a partner start piping with the star tip while you finish crumb coating the other half.

Use a star tip to pipe on green frosting, then blend in blue for an accent. Stick fondant diamond plates into back. If the frosting does not hold the plates well, stick a toothpick into the plate then stick it into the cake.

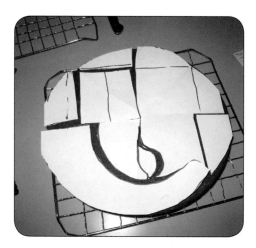

Step 5: The Final Touches

Spread a layer of white frosting on your cake board and toss some toasted coconut around for grass. Add any other finishing touches you like. Add candy corn for spikes on the tail, cinnamon candies for the eyes, and chocolate chips for the toes. We made palm trees using tube cookies with fronds of parsley—this was the first thing every kid wanted so make a small forest if you do it. Grab the camera and enjoy!

Bass Fish Cake

By Tami Chitwood

(tchitwood)

(http://www.instructables.com/id/
How-to-Make-a-Bass-Fish-Cake/)

I made my second sculpted/3D cake and I'm so happy with it! This was made for my nephew who's turning twelve and loves to fish (he said that he "was put on this earth to fish"). He also just joined a junior bass fishing club. The fish itself is made out of Rice Krispie treats, covered in the MMF, and then detailed and hand painted. The cake is strawberry—his favorite—with buttercream. I made the cattails from gum paste. I also made some lures, sinkers, and bobbers and put them on cupcakes as decoration.

Step 1: Mold the Rice Krispie Treats

First, I made a double batch of Rice Krispie treats. I just used the recipe on the box. With a light coating of Crisco on my hands, I molded the treats around dowels into the shapes of the two parts of the fish.

Step 2: Covering the Pieces with Fondant

Next, I made a double batch of marshmallow fondant. Then I rolled out the fondant and covered the treat shapes with it. I then used my fingers and some plastic clay tools to do all the detailing and sculpting.

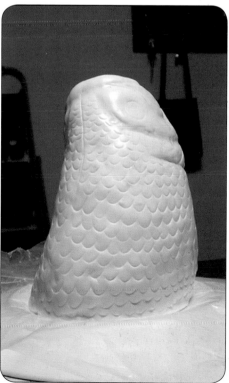

Step 4: Painting the Fish

I painted the large fish parts and the fins separately and then attached the fins with a little bit of water and the help of some toothpicks. I used Wilton gel colors mixed with vodka for the painting. I layered it up in several steps. First was a light greenish brown, then a couple light washes of a green with a little brown mixed in. Then I added the darker green "spots" and finally a little light pink with a touch of gray in and around the mouth.

Step 3: Making the Fins

I then made the fins out of some of the fondant and textured them using the tools. I draped some of the pieces over or up against rolled up paper so that they would dry in the shapes/curves that I wanted.

Step 5: Make Cattails and Grass out of Gum Paste

I forgot to take photos of making the cattails and grass, but I have a photo of them drying. I hung them off of a light fixture to dry. I wrapped heavy wire in green floral tape, molded the brown part out of gum paste, and slid it on. For the grass, I cut out a long strip of gum paste, laid the floral wire down, and then folded the gum paste strip over the wire. Once they were dry, I painted them with the gel color/vodka mixes.

Step 6: Make the Cake Mix

I used a box mix for the cake (strawberry) in a quarter sheet pan. To make the cake a little denser to hold up to the weight of the fish, I used WASC (white almond sour cream) additions and instructions to make the cake.

Once the cake cooled, I attached it to my foil-covered board with some buttercream icing. Next I positioned the fish where I wanted it to be on the cake, marked the area, and then removed the fish. I scooped out a little bit of cake in the areas that I marked so that the fish parts would be inset in the cake a little. I used thick straws (cut down to the height of the cake) as supports where I was going to put the fish parts. Then I piped some icing in the area and put the fish parts back in place.

Icing Recipe
- 2 cups Crisco
- 2 pound bag of powdered sugar
- 4 tablespoons meringue powder
- 2 teaspoons clear vanilla extract/flavor
- 2 teaspoons clear butter flavor
- 1 teaspoon clear almond extract/flavor
- ½ teaspoon salt
- Water

Sift the powdered sugar and meringue powder together into a bowl. In a small bowl or a measuring cup, put in all the flavorings/extracts and then add to that enough water to make the mix ½ cup. Add in the salt and stir until the salt is dissolved. In the mixer bowl, put the Crisco and water/extract mix. Beat on a medium-low speed for about forty seconds, to just get it started mixing. Next, slowly start adding in your powdered sugar/meringue mix while mixing. Once it's all in there, mix on that same slow speed for about a minute. Then just color the icing however you want. I used a little green, lots of royal blue, and a little black.

Step 7: Pipe in the Water

I piped in the water with the buttercream icing using petal tip #104. I started up against the fish parts and just kept going around and around and around.

Step 9: Fishing Tackle Cupcakes

This is an addition I had for my cake. I made some lures, sinkers, and bobbers out of gum paste and hand painted them. When I made the cake, I also made some cupcakes. I piped the icing on them the same way I did the water on the cake, starting with the outer edge of the cupcakes. Then I placed the various fishing tackle items on top as decorations. Here are a few various photos of the making of the tackle and the finished cupcakes.

Step 8: Finish the Cake!

Once the water was all done, I added in the cattails and grass, adding some extra piping around them to help stabilize them. And then it's done!

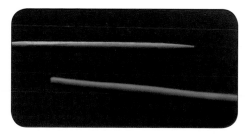

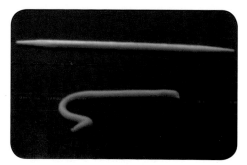

Ladybug and Babybug

By Evren Uzer, Mehtap
Kocaman, and Ayca Beygo
(evrenuzer)
(http://www.instructables.com/
id/ladybug-and-babybug/)

This very tasty and, in our opinion, very cute cake is one of the four cakes that were produced during a one day cake event involving totally amateur participants. These cakes have chocolate cream, labne cheese, and ladyfingers as filling and are covered with white and red whipped cream, M&Ms, and chocolate pieces.

Step 1: Main Frame
Ingredients
- Ladyfingers (400 grams)
- 2 glasses of lukewarm water
- 2 soup spoons of granulated coffee
- 2 packages of cream (200 grams)
- 1 glass water or milk
- 150 grams of cream chocolate
- 100 grams of labne cheese (labneh cheese, or non-salted cream cheese, or sour cream might also work)

- 50 grams cocoa
- 1 package of small chocolate balls

To make our ladybugs, we chose a deep and one small circular bowl for our two ladybugs. Soften your ladyfingers in a coffee and lukewarm water mixture for a very short period of time, and then place them into your bowls (lined with a piece of stretch film to make it easier to take your cake out of the bowl later). Make sure not to keep the ladyfingers in the coffee/water mixture for too long, as they will get soft quickly. You want them to be shapeable but not falling apart.

Step 2: Filling
Now, mix the chocolate cream and the labne cheese, and add the mixture into your bowls with the ladyfingers. Add another layer of softened ladyfingers and then another layer of chocolate/cheese mixture. Continue repeating this layering pattern until you reach the top of the bowls. Then, add a thin layer of cocoa and cover them with transparent stretch film.

30

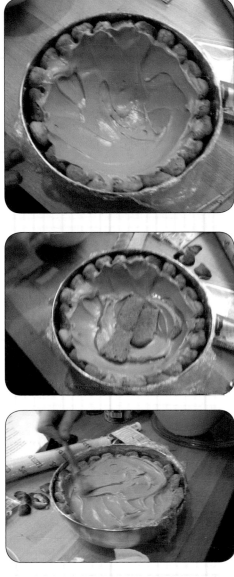

Step 3: Freezing and Outer Decoration

Place your bowls with the ladyfingers and chocolate/cheese mixture into the freezer for an hour. In the meantime, mix your whipped cream with some red food color. After an hour, take your ladybugs out of the freezer, take both of them out of their bowls, and cover them up with the red whipped cream. Then, place chocolate pieces in one corner to form the face.

Step 4: Face and the Final Touch

Make the eyes with whipped cream and add one piece of chocolate in the center. Place dark colored M&Ms on the top. Add some antennas and you're done!

Fire-Breathing Dragon Cake

By Margaret Wilkes
(kitchenwench)
(http://www.instructables.com/
id/Fire-Breathing-Dragon-Cake!!/)

I first saw this idea in a children's magazine and decided to make it for my younger brother's fifth knight-themed birthday party. With two ordinary 9" cakes, frosting, and a few other easy-to-find candies, you can create a very realistic dragon!

Step 1: Ingredients and Equipment

- 2 9" cakes
- 6 cups of frosting (more or less, depending on how thick you like your icing), your choice of color
- 8 Keebler chocolate-covered graham crackers
- 8 Sunkist fruit gems
- 2 Sunkist fruit slices
- 2 blue Fruit Roll-Ups
- 1 red Fruit Roll-Up
- 1 yellow Fruit Roll-Up
- 1 marshmallow
- 2 chocolate chips
- 2 Hershey's kisses
- 2 wooden skewers

You will want all your fruit gems, slices, and icing to be color coordinated—I chose orange candies and yellow icing, but you can do whatever colors will match the plates or napkins you will have at the party.

Step 2: Preparation

Take a serrated bread knife and cut the middle part out of all the rectangular crackers, so that you have two triangular pieces out of each one. Next, slice all of the fruit gems in half.

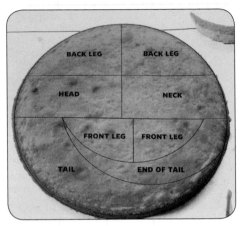

Step 3: Assembly

Take one of your 9″ round cakes and slice it in half. Take your frosting and spread some on one half, then place the other half on top, and place the whole thing on a cardboard cake board or aluminum-foil-covered cardboard. Next, you will cut up the remaining cake. The diagram in the picture shows exactly how to do it. Don't worry if it isn't exact—you can always make a small piece look bigger with icing.

Step 4: Icing

Next, assemble the cake pieces according to the picture, trimming any pieces if necessary. Now, you will frost Mr. Dragon. I find that using a flat icing tip in your full icing bag works wonders on those difficult, moist, and crummy parts, and once you've covered up the crumbs, you can use your spatula to smooth things over. This method keeps those crumbs from showing up in your icing.

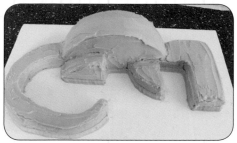

the skewer, trim off the edges bat-wing style. Repeat for other wing. Make sure not to stick these in until right before serving, because they are heavy and will sag over time. For the fire, trim your yellow and red roll-ups into curvy, twisty pieces, and position near mouth. And, there you have it!

Step 5: Decorate!

Now, you will decorate the dragon! First, to make the dragon look like he is scaly, use a child's marker cap to imprint the design onto the creamy frosting. Arrange the graham crackers along his back and tail; place fruit gems and slices as his toes and on his head to look like eyebrows. Press the Hershey's kisses pointy-side-in onto the end of his snout, and cut the marshmallow in half, place the two pieces where the dragon's eyes will be, and place the chocolate chips on top of the two marshmallow halves.

Step 6: Wings and Fire

To make his wings, you'll need a skewer and a blue fruit roll-up. Trim off a corner of the roll-up to keep them from looking too bulky, and after rolling it up

Section 2

Foods

This fun party cake was made with regular Funfetti cake mix and a few cheap and easy household ingredients. The prep time is minimal, and the results are sure to elicit lots of "oohs" and "aahs" from your party guests!

Ingredients
- Cake mix
- Fruit Roll-Ups
- Orange Jell-O
- Sweetened, shredded coconut
- Kiwi
- Frosting
- Chopsticks
- Soy sauce

Step 1: Make "Salmon Roe" Jell-O Fish Eggs

Use a single box of orange Jell-O and prepare it according the mold instructions on the box. I make mine in a refrigerator egg tray, but you could likely also use the foam carton that the eggs come in. I sprayed the tray with cooking spray first so that the "eggs" would come out of the mold unscathed. Put them in the fridge for at least three hours to set. This step would be best done the night before.

Step 2: Bake Your Cakes

Simply bake a cake from a store-bought mix of your choice using two 9" round pans. After baking, set aside to cool completely.

Step 3: Frost Your Cake

Using any sort of white frosting, put your two cooled cake layers together and frost them completely.

Step 4: Cover Top with Coconut "Rice"

Sprinkle the top with a nice, thick layer of sweetened, shredded coconut, avoiding the very center.

Step 5: Apply Fruit Roll-Up "Seaweed"

Using a paring knife, cut green Fruit Roll-Up slices to fit the outside of the cake and carefully stick it to the frosting the entire way around the cake. Be sure to apply it quickly before it becomes hot and sticky.

Step 6: Make "Ginger" and "Wasabi"

You can layer thin slices of orange and red Fruit Roll-Ups for a nice ginger color. After sticking them together, wrinkle them up a bit and set them beside the cake on the plate. Peel a kiwi and cut it slightly over the halfway mark, so that you have one larger piece and one smaller piece. Cut notches out of it randomly to resemble a blob of wasabi. Place it next to the "ginger" on the plate.

Step 7: Apply Your Salmon Roe

Dip your Jell-O mold in hot water for a few moments to loosen the eggs and then very carefully jiggle it around and slide them out. Using a spatula, slide them onto the center of the cake. I used four because that fit best, but yours may be smaller. Simply use however many you think look best.

Step 8: Garnish with Chopstick and Soy Sauce

Add a pair of wooden chopsticks to the top and a couple packets of soy sauce next to the ginger and wasabi for authenticity. I even used a piece of the plastic grass from a real sushi order!

Cake Fries

By Lisa Trifiro

(imnopeas)

(http://www.instructables.com/
id/Cake-Fries/)

What's better than a nice, hot and crispy French fry? Uh, nothing—but these faux French fries made from pound cake are pretty darn tasty! These dessert fries are the perfect addition to any BBQ or summer bash. They are served with a faux raspberry ketchup for your dipping pleasure. Alternatively, you can use regular red frosting.

Step 1: Ingredients and Tools

- 1 Sara Lee Pound Cake
- 2 containers fresh raspberries
- 2 tablespoons lemon juice
- 4 tablespoons confectioner's sugar
- 1 zigzag knife (a.k.a. crinkle cutter), or you can use a regular knife for straight-edge fries
- Strainer
- Bowl
- Baking sheet
- Fry liner paper

Step 2: Cut Cake into Crinkle Fries

First, slice the ends of each side of the pound cake and save them for later or discard. Next, use a zigzag knife to cut the pound cake lengthwise into regular size pieces. Lastly, use the zigzag knife to cut the pound cake vertically into strips resembling fries. Leave the brown part on each end of the fries for an added realistic effect.

Step 3: Make the Raspberry Ketchup

To make the raspberry ketchup, rinse the raspberries under cold water. Next, place them in the blender with a few tablespoons of lemon juice. Purée the raspberries until they are broken up and smooth. Next, add 2 tablespoons at a time of confectioner's sugar. Purée the raspberry mixture again. Repeat.

Place the mixture into a strainer over a bowl. Use a spatula and press the puree down into the strainer until only the seeds remain. Pour the raspberry ketchup into a ketchup bottle and place some into a small dipping bowl.

Step 4: Broil Fries

Pre-heat the broiler. Place the cake fries on a baking sheet. Place fries under the broil for ten to fifteen seconds on each side or until lightly browned. Place the light on in the oven so you can watch them brown. Do not leave fries unattended or they will burn.

Step 5: Happiness!

Place cake fries in a fry cone or basket with liner. Pour raspberry ketchup into a bottle and place some on the side for dipping. Serve immediately. If they sit out for too long, they may dry out.

Giant Peep Cake

By Sarah James
(scoochmaroo)
(http://www.instructables.com/
id/Giant-Peep-Cake/)

You know spring has sprung when Peeps hit the shelves. Those little marshmallow chicks herald longer days, warmer weather, and the promise of a future trip to the dentist. Celebrate their reemergence with the Giant Peep, a cake that is all of spring baked into an homage to everyone's* favorite April treat.

This Giant Peep Cake is 200 times the size of a normal peep, which is important, as it contains a surprise clutch of Peeps within.

Step 1: Materials

I originally got this idea from an issue of *Food Network* Magazine, but decided they had really missed an opportunity with their Peep Cake. I took their recipe one step further and filled my Giant Peep Cake with a brood of store-bought marshmallow Peeps!

Cake

Use your favorite cake recipe for the body of the cake. You'll want to double it up. I used two box mixes! If you want to know a secret, often when I "test-kitchen" cake recipes at work, I'll throw in one that's straight from a box.

It's usually everyone's favorite, which is part disappointment and part relief, as it means when I need to throw together a cake super quick, no one will mind if I make one from a box. Shh . . .

Frosting

The frosting here really tastes like melted down peeps. I recommend trying this, although the texture can be a bit tricky, and a buttercream, or even pre-packaged frosting, would be much easier to work with. But if you're game, try this:

- 1.5 cups sugar
- ½ teaspoon cream of tartar
- 3 large egg whites
- 1 teaspoon vanilla extract
- 1 teaspoon yellow food coloring
- Yellow sugar
- Chocolate for eyes

Pans

To shape the body you'll want to use a variety of baking vessels:

- 9" × 13" baking pan
- 1-quart oven safe bowl
- 2.5-quart oven safe bowl

Make sure to grease and flour the pans well.

Innards

This recipe makes a solid, delicious, giant peep cake. But if you're feeling zany, you can hollow it out and fill it with tiny peeps and surprise and delight your guests! I was able to fit fifteen peeps in the cavity I created.

---

*Not actually everyone.

46

Step 2: Make the Cake

Mix up your double batch of cake. Distribute among your three greased and floured pans. Bake at 350°F for 35–40 minutes for the pan and small bowl and 50–55 minutes for the larger bowl. Let cakes cool in their vessels for 15 minutes, and then unmold and let cool completely.

Step 3: Shape the Cake

Once the cakes are cool, it's time to carve them into shape. Cut the corners off of the rectangle and reserve pieces for the tail and beak. Level the tops of the bowl cakes to create a flat surface. Eat the scraps immediately. (You're welcome.)

If you want a hollow cake, use the large round cake to mark out its placement on the rectangular cake. Then cut out a circle about 1" inside this mark (see picture on following page). Cut a circle inside the large round cake and also the small round cake if desired. I kept the smallest circle to place on top and add height to the crown.

Step 4: Assemble the Cake

I put thin strips of waxed paper under each side of the cake so that when I went to frost it later, I could be as messy as I wanted to be. Then, I gently slid out the waxed paper with all of the excess frosting on it, leaving a clean finish. Place the large round cake upside down on the other end of the rectangle (over the hole if you decided to cut one). Place the small round cake upside down on the large round (again, aligning holes if you decided to hollow it out).

If you've decided to stuff your cake with peeps, now is the time. If you've cut the middle out of the small round, place this on top as well. Trim another triangle to make a beak and use a skewer to secure to the face. You'll use frosting to fill out the rest of the beak shape. The real trick to getting the shape right here is not to center each of the round cakes on top of the other, but to line up the backs of the rounds so it looks like the peep is pulling its head back slightly. This took me a few tries to get right. Use toothpicks or skewers to attach two of the triangle corners to the short end of the rectangle cake to form a tail.

Step 5: Frosting

To make the frosting:

- Create simple syrup of the sugar, cream of tartar, and ⅔ cup of water, by heating in a saucepan until dissolved.
- Whip egg whites with a mixer until frothy.
- Slowly beat in the simple syrup, then increase the speed of the mixer to beat into stiff peaks, about 7–8 minutes.
- Beat in vanilla and food coloring until well combined.

Step 6: Decorate the Cake

Frost the cake with a "crumb coat" first —a thin layer of frosting to keep all of the crumbs intact. Since we did so much carving on the cake, it's sure to be crumbly, and we want to contain the mess as much as possible. Once the cake has been coated, start piling on a thick layer of frosting. Use this to smooth out the shape of your final peep, and build out the beak and the tail.

Coat the cake with a thick dusting of the yellow sanding sugar. The only way I was able to get it on the undersides of the beak and tail was to sort of throw the sugar up and at it. It was pretty fun, if not terribly effective. For the eyes, I melted some chocolate and poured

little disks. If you have chocolate wafers, use those instead. Remove the strips of waxed paper and serve.

Step 7: Enjoy!

Since I had all these peeps, I decided to stage a few scenarios. When the cake was cut open, all of the peeps inside spilled out in a manner that appeared to frighten the other peeps. The inside peeps them proceeded to chase the outside peeps as the outside peeps fled in terror into the open mouths of my coworkers. Yum!

Section 3

Games

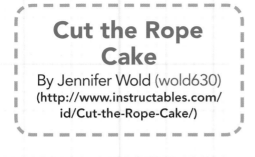

- Couplers
- Toothpicks
- Cake board/cardboard for putting the cake on
- Waxed paper
- Food coloring
- Spreading knife
- Fondant
- Some creativity!

"Deliver candy to Om Nom!" I hear this phrase all the time. Both of my boys love Cut the Rope, so for my son's third birthday, he decided he wanted a cake with Om Nom—his favorite character, of course!

There are many beautiful and amazing cakes out there that have been covered/decorated with fondant. I am sort of a fondant hater. Mainly because it tastes horrible! I have bought fondant and made (marshmallow) fondant from scratch with the same outcome. The cake tastes great but the fondant has to be picked off and thrown away.

Now, if you don't have kids, you might not think this is a big deal; but when kids don't like the taste of fondant, and you have to take it off of their cake, and all the frosting goes with it . . . well, there are many, many unwanted tears to deal with!

So, in an attempt to satisfy my little birthday boy, I tried my best to smooth out buttercream frosting instead of using fondant: a usual event for me when making cakes. With that said, there is no better way to create characters and/or graphic decorations than to use fondant. All of the dots and characters on this cake are made using store bought fondant.

Ingredients and Equipment

- 2 9" square cakes of your choice
- Buttercream frosting—white, green, and blue
- Piping bags
- 2 #3 decorating tips

Step 1: Sculpting

This is pretty simple to explain. Get out fondant. Add food coloring of your choice and knead until the color is uniform throughout. I like using Wilton icing colors because the color turns out so rich. I have tried using the cheap liquid drop version with less luck. The color just isn't as vibrant in my opinion.

Years ago in painting class, I was told to never use the paint right out of the tube. The paint should be mixed in some way with another color. I would recommend this when using food coloring just so it's not so typical. I understand that a color might be perfect so don't change it if you don't have to, but it's fun to experiment and get some new colors that you've never tried. Optional, of course, but you might surprise yourself. Don't be afraid!

The hard part is sculpting characters and decorations you need. Trying and trying again is the best method. Using tools can be helpful—a knife, toothpicks, ceramic tools (clean please), cups, glasses, cookie cutters, etc.

Use your fingers to smooth out the fondant, making sure there are no visible cracks. Use a tiny bit of water to get pieces to stick to one another. If you need very thin pieces, roll out fondant between pieces of waxed paper, coating the fondant lightly with cornstarch so it doesn't stick. When I cut out the green circles, I left them out for a while so they were stiff and easier to work with. Once they sit on the frosting a while they get soft again, so don't worry about having crispy pieces on your cake!

I will try to briefly explain how to make each character/design:

- Om Nom—I decided after Om Nom was complete to enter this cake and start taking pictures, so I don't have good pictures of the process to make him. He is two separate pieces. I started with a basic half sphere, made the top of his head a little more pointed, and indented the bottom part so his head would sit well on the base, or bottom half, of his body. Make a small little snake shape, rounded at the end, for the top of his head. Use a dab of water to stick it on. For his eyes, I just pressed out some white fondant, but you could roll it with a rolling pin if you want. Get the shape you want and again stick the pieces on with a dab of water. Make two tiny black dots to complete the eyes. To make the bottom of Om Nom, start with another half sphere. Using a table knife cut a square out of the front to make his front legs. You will have to shape them and smooth out the fondant where you cut. Make two cubes and stick them on the sides to make his back legs. Make four wide rounded triangles and put them underneath the top piece to make his teeth.

- Stars—If you have a star cookie cutter that is the right size, it would be great for this. I shaped them with my fingers, since I don't have a cookie cutter, and rounded the points. Make a small thin white snake and press it down flat. Edge the stars with the white to give them detail and add white dots.
- Balloons—Using light blue fondant, make a circle that is somewhat rounded and not completely flat. Add a small triangle to one of the sides for the air spout. Using dark blue fondant, make rounded squares and add them to the center. Cut more rounded squares in half and put four on each side of each balloon.
- Candy—Make a ball with yellow fondant and press it down to make flat sides. Make long red triangles

and adhere four of them, with points meeting in the center.
- Spiders—Make a circle out of black fondant. Using a toothpick, make indents all around the edge. Press out white circles and black dots for the eyes. These are simple!
- Spikes—Using brownish fondant, roll a thin snake and press it down flat. Make several gray diamonds and stick them along the brown snake.
- Circles—To make the green circles, I rolled the fondant out as thin as possible and cut them with the top of a small shot glass. Let them dry out to make them easier to stick on the cake.

Don't skimp on the details. It will take longer but the outcome will be well worth it!

Place the bottom cake on a cake base of some kind. Mine was a reflective cardboard square. Cut thin strips of waxed paper to put under the bottom edges of the cake so as to not smear frosting all over the base. Spread a generous layer of buttercream frosting on top. Place the second cake upside down on the bottom cake.

I always use white frosting for the layers and then mix the frosting color for the outside. That way I know exactly how much is needed for the middle, instead of guessing and having way too much white left over. You want to make sure you have enough to cover the entire cake.

Mix the remaining frosting with desired food coloring(s) and place in piping bags if necessary. Spread main color evenly and smoothly on all cake sides using a spreading knife.

Step 2: Layer Cake

Bake two 9" square cakes of your choice according to directions. Cool on wire racks. While cakes are cooling, make frosting.

Buttercream

- 1 cup butter, room temperature (you can substitute vegetable shortening if you prefer a firmer texture)
- ½ cup water
- 1 teaspoon vanilla extract
- 2 pounds powdered sugar
- 4 tablespoons butter, melted

In the bowl of a stand mixer, beat butter, water, powdered sugar, and vanilla until smooth. Add melted butter and continue to beat until smooth, scraping down sides as needed. After both cakes are baked and cooled, cut each top off to make the cakes level.

Step 3: Decorate

You've done all the work, here is the fun part—decorate! Place fondant green circles in an alternating pattern on the top and sides. Cut in half if necessary to go on the edges. Using a piping bag with a #3 piping tip and white frosting, pipe small lines on all edges of the cake to resemble stitching. Add on the rest of the desired decorations and fondant pieces where you want them. I used many toothpicks to stand pieces up to give the cake some dimension. If you are not serving the cake immediately, let the cake sit uncovered about thirty minutes to make sure the frosting is stiff (so plastic wrap won't stick). Then cover with plastic wrap to keep the cake fresh.

Step 4: Birthday Time!

Watch happily as your little birthday boy (or girl) devours the cake that they wouldn't stop talking about!

Rubik's Battenberg Cake
By Vicky McDonalds
(stasty)
(http://www.instructables.com/id/Rubiks-Battenburg-Cake/)

Why make this cake? The Rubik's cube is close to my heart, as I am a child of the eighties, and it always brings me back to a time of joy and wonder. It's hard to imagine kids today being as fascinated as I was by such a simple but clever toy. I wanted to make a cake that epitomizes this ingenious and timeless invention. I knew it would have to be a clever cake that would make you question how it was made. Thankfully, I had the help of my other half and his engineering brain to assist with the planning and general math of this cake. It took an entire day to make but was definitely worthwhile, especially when we cut the first slice.

Ingredients

One Basic Battenberg—White-Colored and Yellow-Colored Cake
- 6 oz of butter
- 6 oz of castor sugar
- 3 eggs
- 6 oz of self-rising flour
- 2 drops of almond essence (optional for the white)
- Zest of half an unwaxed lemon (optional for the yellow)
- A few drops of yellow food coloring

One Basic Battenberg—Red-Colored and Orange-Colored Cake
- 6 oz of butter
- 6 oz of castor sugar
- 3 eggs
- 6 oz of self-rising flour
- A few drops of red food coloring
- Zest of half an orange (optional for the orange)
- A few drops of orange food coloring

One Basic Battenberg—Blue-Colored and Green-Colored cake
- 6 oz of butter
- 6 oz of castor sugar
- 3 eggs
- 6 oz of self-rising flour
- A few drops of blue food coloring
- A few drops of green food coloring

To Finish
- 14 oz of blackcurrant jam, sieved
- 14 oz of plain white marzipan to cover the entire cake
- 2 oz of icing sugar for rolling out the marzipan

Tools
- Weighing scales
- Electric beaters
- Large mixing bowl
- Battenberg tin
- Wire rack for cooling
- Large serrated knife
- Saucepan
- Sieve
- Rolling pin
- Pastry brush
- Ruler

Step 1: Baking the Cakes

Pre-heat the oven 180° Celsius. Grease and flour a Battenberg tin. My Battenberg tin was 8" × 6" and had four individual sections to put in the different colors. You'll need to make three cakes, and each cake will comprise two of the colors needed—white/ yellow, then red/orange, and finally blue/green. Cream together the butter and the sugar until it becomes light and creamy. Gradually add the beaten eggs. Then, carefully fold in the sieved flour.

Next, split the mixture to make the two different colors. Take half of the mixture out, and place it in another bowl. Add a few drops of food coloring to one batch. To the other half, add a few drops of a different food coloring. For the white sections of the cake, I slightly over-beat the egg mixture and didn't add any coloring. This achieved a pale off-white effect.

Spoon the mixture into the separate sections of the tin. Place in the oven for 30 to 35 minutes. To test if it's ready, place a clean knife through the center— the knife should come out clean when it is fully cooked. If the cake rises over the tin, use a serrated knife to even off the top. Let the cake cool in the tin; once fully cooled, remove the cake from the tin and place it on a wire rack. Repeat twice more, using the same method, ingredients, and remaining food colors for the red/orange and blue/green cakes.

Optionally, you might want to flavor the cakes as well as color them. I used lemon zest for the yellow, orange zest for the orange, and vanilla for the white. You want to find complimentary flavors that will work as a cake, so it's probably best to resist the temptation to put mint flavoring in the green, as it could taint the whole cake.

Step 2: The Grid

Decide on the color combinations. It is important that each slice is different. Each section overlaps so each slice of the cake reveals a differing combination. The picture shows the map we created that would guarantee that each slice was different to the one previous. Note: I've used the color black on the map to represent white in the cake, because white looked clearer as the background of the spreadsheet.

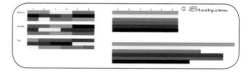

Step 3: Cutting Guide

With a ruler, draw out a cutting grid that is the size of the tin. (Our tin was 8" × 6".) We drew our grid with pen and ruler on a sheet of A4 paper and measured all of our cakes piece with this. Cut out the cake pieces using your paper grid. We did this all together, so we were left with deconstructed cake pieces of different sizes.

Step 4: Building the Cake

Roll out a long even slab of marzipan. We rolled ours out to be about 10″ × 26″ (10″ = 8″ plus another 2″ spare to work with; 26″ = 4″ × 6″ plus another 2″). This will depend on your cake and tin size. Place the jam in a saucepan and warm over a low heat. Next, sieve the warm jam into a separate bowl to remove any seeds in the jam. Begin with the bottom layer. With a pastry brush, coat the entire outside of each cake cube and arrange them on top of the marzipan with the unjammed face pointing outwards.

Step 5: Sticking It All Together

Continue building using your spreadsheet to figure out where all the pieces go and applying the jam to stick it together.

Step 6: Wrapping in Marzipan

Once you have all three layers of cake in place, ensure that the outside of each piece of cake is covered in jam so the marzipan will stick. Gently place the marzipan over the cake and cut off the spare on the edges.

Step 7: Slicing

To cut the cake, use the grid to figure out the correct place to slice to ensure you reveal a different colored slice. Voilà!

Rubik's Cube Cake

By J'Aime Salisbury
(asyrith)
(http://www.instructables.com/
id/Make-the-tiles/)

Oh, yes. The ever infuriating Rubik's Cube. No doubt we have all spent a good deal of time on our favorite 1980s toy. Some of us are naturally gifted . . . alas, most of us are not. Regardless, I think we all have a special place in our hearts for the cube. It is a timeless symbol of geekiness! Let us not forget it! In this Instructable, I will teach you how to pay tribute to this awesome cube. It's simple to do and anyone can achieve the awesomeness that is the final project. Wow your friends and read on!

Step 1: Bake the Cake

First, you need to chose a type of cake to bake. It really doesn't have to be any particular kind for this cake. Use your favorite recipe or box mix and double it.

Ingredients

- Recipe or cake mix of your choosing doubled
- 9" × 9" cake pans (You can either have three or you can bake the cake in shifts.)
- Nonstick spray
- Your choice of frosting
- Your choice of filling
- A lot of food coloring in red, green, yellow, and blue. (This will be for the squares.)
- Either black food coloring or dark chocolate ganache. Depends on your taste. This will cover the cube. Black food coloring tends to dye mouths purple and a ganache can be shinier. However, you might achieve more of a black by using food coloring. More on this later.
- Fondant—I highly recommend making your own marshmallow fondant. It's simply, delicious, and looks very professional.

So, get started baking your cake. You will want to prepare double your recipe for this cake. I like to use box mixes because they are no fuss and turn out delicious. I do, however, think it makes a world of a difference to prepare your own frosting. Pour your batter into designated square pans. If you have to rotate one pan to bake all three, it won't hurt, but it will take longer. Bake until the cakes lightly bounce back when you touch them or just before. Note: Cakes actually continue baking in their pans, even when you pull them out of the oven. To get a really moist cake, pull the cake out just before it looks done and it should cook to perfection. In my opinion, nothing beats a moist cake. Another thing I suggest to maintain moistness is to put some cling wrap over the cake when it cools a bit. It will collect the condensation and keep your cake very moist! I usually only do this for cakes that have a tendency to dry out more, such as chocolate, but do what you like!

Step 2: Prepare the Marshmallow Fondant

For this step, you will need:

- A bag of good-quality, mini marshmallows. I say good quality because I have used discount marshmallows that refused to melt!
- 2–5 tablespoons of water. (This isn't exact. You may need more or less. You just want your fondant to be workable.)
- 1 bag of powdered sugar (or icing sugar)
- Crisco or anything nonstick for your hands and counter. (Things *will* get sticky!)

Melt your marshmallows and add about 2 tablespoons of water in a large, microwave-safe bowl. Put the bowl in the microwave for 30 second intervals. After every 30 seconds, open the microwave and stir the mixture until it is fully melted. This should take about 2½ minutes. When melted, pour about three quarters of the powdered sugar on top of the marshmallow.

Now things get messy! Grease your counters *well*. Be liberal with the amount of shortening you spread around. Be sure to get it on your hands and wrists as well. I know it feels weird! Just go with it and you'll have nice and soft hands when you're finished. Start kneading your mixture like it was bread dough. You now have discovered the stickiest thing known to man! Contemplate your plans for world domination with such stickiness and keep on kneading. Abandon your plans and keep kneading. Add the rest of the powdered sugar. If you're sticky, add more grease; if your fondant is tearing, add a little water. You will want to work it until it becomes a smooth, elastic ball. Now you want to break it off into little groups for your colors. You will need six separate balls for each color. The best way to color these is to get individual baggies for them and drip the food coloring into the bag. Now you get to knead some more! Knead and add color until you get the color you're looking for. Continue with each color. Set aside.

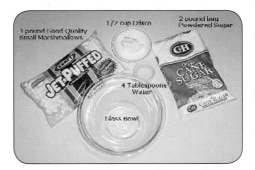

Step 3: "Square" the Cakes

After your cakes have completely cooled, you will want to level and square them. You'll notice that the tops and sides are rounded. To get the sides square, use a paper template to get even results. To level the top, you can use a cake leveler or you can find something to use as a mark for even knife leveling. In the picture below, a box of powdered sugar happens to be the perfect height for such a project.

Step 4: Begin to Form the Cube!

First thing you need to decide is how your cube is going to sit. I prefer the "in progress" look of the cube, but you can have it be a correctly aligned cube if you so desire. Put the filling of your choice in between the layers to assure stickiness and added yumminess! The kind of filling is totally up to you. Now . . . stand back and admire your work thus far.

The next step is to cover your cake in a "crumb coat" with your frosting. Don't feel bad when this looks ugly. That's why it's a crumb coat. Just make sure to evenly coat your cube and let it dry before you move on to the next coat of frosting. Frost it one more time so that it looks nice and clean. Basically, we just don't want to see crumbs. Also, get it as smooth as you can manage.

Now, we're going to transform our pale cake into a black cube of awesome! There are two ways to do this:

1. Use black food coloring. If you do this, you will have a very black cake and a purple tongue when you eat it. *Do not mix with frosting.* If you do, you shall be very sad at a very gray cake. Instead, after your second coat of frosting is dry, paint on the food coloring. Get a nice even coat.
2. Use chocolate ganache. This tastes terrific, but gives a dark brown instead of a true black. It depends on what you prefer.

How to Make Ganache

The ingredients you need are:

- 1 pound bittersweet chocolate, chopped
- 1 pint heavy cream
- 5⅓ oz unsalted butter

Bring cream and butter to a simmer. Pour over chocolate and stir/whisk until melted and smooth.

Make sure your cube is evenly coated and allow it to dry completely before moving on.

Step 5: Make the Tiles!

Now, get out those six baggies you should have.

- White
- Yellow
- Orange
- Red
- Blue
- Green

You now want to roll these out and cut them into small squares. One should equal slightly less than a third of the cake, so that when you have nine on there, it will look right. To do this, roll out the color into a rough square and hold it up to the cake. If it looks about right, cut the colored square into nine equal parts. Do this for each color.

Step 6: Tiles and *Assembly*!

Time to apply your tiles! If you have a cube handy, get it out and scramble it to your liking and then apply your tiles accordingly. Paint the backs of each of your tiles with a small amount of water and apply to the cake. Patience, young Skywalker. This will take some time.

Step 7: Clean It Up!

Now, brush over your tiles with some water to give the cube a nice, clean look. And you're done! Put your real cube next to your cake one and admire your great job!

Moving Tank Birthday Cake

By Dave Spencer
(dave spencer)
(http://www.instructables.com/
id/Tank-birthday-cake/)

We were just on vacation at Disney so I didn't want to get too elaborate due to time constraints. My son asked for a tank cake for his birthday. I'm sure he would have been happy with a cake with a picture of a tank on it or a model tank. But I would not have been happy. First, I decided that the turret would rotate. That is pretty easy. I toyed with the idea of having it shoot something (what says happy birthday more than getting shot in the face with whipped cream?). That idea got shelved as soon as I imagined the look on my wife's face. To up the difficulty level, I decided to make the gun go up and down as the turret rotated. Imagine wife smiling.

Step 1: The Mechanism
I started with some scrap parts I had laying around, mostly stainless steel. The stainless sheet metal was the same piece of scrap I used for the volcano cake last year. Since it was not going to shoot anything, I started with a solid stainless barrel, welded a bracket and a pivot onto it, and fixed it to the turret pan.

By the way, nothing puts a smile on my face more than describing how I make cakes with a welder.

To make the gun travel up and down, I decided to make a rod and cam type system. I welded a guide tube to the turret pan and made a "cam" of sorts out of a metal disk that I heated with a torch and bent randomly. I then fixed this to a tube that would act as a bushing for the turret pan rotation. I had a slow turning motor sitting around the house, which I mounted to a piece of wood as a base. I welded legs to the cam and drilled them into the wooden base. I set it all on a bit of an angle so the tank would be tilted slightly when done. You can see that the turret pan warped a bit during welding, but I was not too concerned and I did not bother to correct it. The push rod was installed to slide along the cam and to raise the barrel. The last thing I did was put on the barrel guard. I used perforated steel for two reasons: One was that it would be really easy to bend a slight curve into it, and two was so the icing would have something to adhere to.

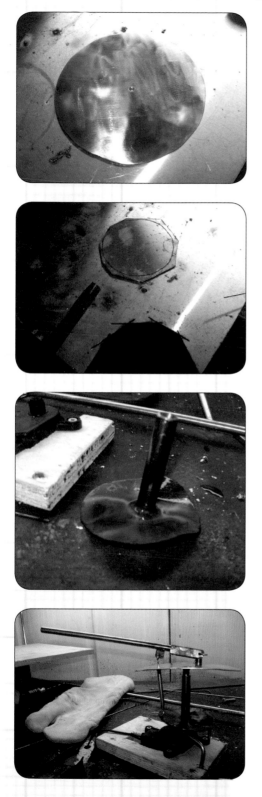

Step 2: The Cake

The turret pan was hot glued to another piece of wood that was to act as the base. Anything that would touch cake that was not stainless was covered with tin foil. I made four cakes for this. One cake was baked in a pot the same diameter as the turret pan. A little bit of carving and I had my turret shape and clearance for the barrel and mechanism. The other cakes were baked in a 9" × 11" pan. Once cooled, the rounded tops were sliced off. These tops were used for the ground. The main parts of the cake were carved to fit around the mechanism and stacked to create the rough tank shape. All pieces were "glued" together with icing. A bit of carving with a sharp knife and it was starting to look like a tank.

tread in, I stuck a piece of wax paper on top, flipped the whole thing over, peeled off the new top side of the wax paper, used the other strip of wax paper still stuck to it to move it to the cake, placed it on the cake, and then peeled the wax paper away.

One bit of foresight I had was to make the turret easily removable. This helped in decorating more than I can express. I perched the turret on a pitcher, so it would not tip over on the push rod or the axle, and decorated it there. The stainless barrel was wrapped with fondant and a little bit of detail was put on, like a hatch with a periscope. Wheels were added on the side—these were just icing rolled flat and cut out with various sized cups and caps. The camouflage was added by smooshing random shapes. All detail is stuck in place by simply wetting the area you want to fix it to. The last step was to crumble up some cookies to make the dirt the tank was driving on. That's all folks!

Step 3: The Icing

I planned to use fondant icing right from the start. This was my second attempt at using the stuff. I wish I could take a course on the application of fondant because it really can't be as hard to work with as I find it to be. What a pain in the butt this icing is! To get the fondant to stick to the cake, you need to ice it with regular icing. It is way easier to ice if you freeze the cake first. It is way easier to freeze the cake if you check the dimensions of your freezer prior to building the base! I had to shuffle a lot of food around, but I eventually got it to fit. Oh well, this was a seat of the pants project to begin with.

I mixed colors into the icing as I just bought one big white tub of fondant. The fondant needs to be rolled onto wax paper because it is quite sticky. It even sticks pretty well to the wax paper. I found this to be to my advantage in some cases as I rolled out the tracks. After I used a piece of wood to put the

Section 4

Movies

Rocket Cake (for *Toy Story* Party)

By Simone Graham
(GreatFun4Kidz)
(http://www.instructables.com/id/
Rocket-Cake-for-Toy-Story-Party/)

Here's how to make a gorgeous-but-easy Rocket Cake (made originally for my son's *Toy Story* Party).

Step 1: Method

Triple-recipe of chocolate cake mix, baked in a roasting dish lined with baking paper. (1) Cut off the two corners to form the body of the rocket, then trim the remaining triangles of cake and flip them round to form the rocket fins. Ice the main body blue (with butter cream icing, of course). Ice the fins red. Use the gel colors to produce vibrant color. Slice the bottom off a couplet ice cream cone and poke into the base of the rocket to create the exhaust

Decorate and make pretty. I used the easy-squeeze Queen icing writing tubes and sweets. To create a burst of jet flame, melt orange barley sugar sweets in the oven, on a tray lined with baking paper. When the sweets melt and run together, remove quickly from the oven and use a knife to pull the melted sweets into the shape you want. It will harden and cool quickly; before it becomes brittle, use your hands to refine the shape. Poke into the base of the cake as shown.

Simple, but very effective!

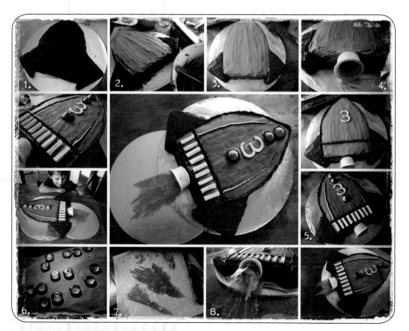

Yoda Head Cake

By Tami Chitwood
(tchitwood)
(http://www.instructables.com/
id/Yoda-Head-Cake/)

I'm an artist who has recently gotten into cake decorating and has also fallen in love with it! I'm currently taking beginner cake decorating classes and hoping to land a job at a bakery. I decided to try making my first sculpted cake and chose Yoda as the subject. It was so much fun. I've found my passion! This is a red velvet cake (with Rice Krispie treats for the ears) covered in fondant. I tried to get as much detail as I could. I wanted to finish the bust with fondant clothing over the neck area and covering the pan and plate, but I ran out of time and fondant. Yoda was very yummy! Everyone said it was sad to cut into him, but we went to the dark side that night. Hopefully I will have time soon to continue the *Star Wars* theme with another sculpted cake.

I was so into making this cake that I forgot to take more photos while I was making it, but here's the written story of how I made the cake.

Step 1

First, I printed out lots of reference photos of Yoda from as many different angles as I could find.

Step 2

Then I baked the cakes. I used two box mixes of red velvet cake, altering/adding to each mix to make the cake stronger so it would hold up to the stacking and carving and fondant better. I made four 8" rounds. Once they were cooled, I stacked them up with white buttercream icing in between the layers. I then put the stacked cake into the freezer for a while so that it would be easier to carve.

Step 3

While the cake was in the freezer, I made the Rice Krispie treats and then molded each ear around some take-out chopsticks.

Step 4

Once the cake was about half-frozen, I looked at my reference photos and just started carving out the basic shape with a knife. I scooped out some cake on the sides to make them the same size around as the base of the ears, so that the ears would be inset a little into the cake and hold up more easily.

78

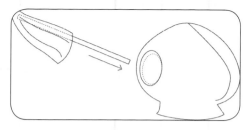

Step 5

Once the carving was done and I had the ears on, I crumb coated it with vanilla buttercream. There are a couple photos I had taken of it after the crumb coating.

Step 6

Then I made the fondant (marshmallow fondant) and covered the cake. The eyes and most of the nose are fondant. I added the eyes separately. First, I made the white oval, then I made and attached the eyelids. I used clay sculpting/carving tools for all the details, wrinkles, etc.

Step 7

Then the last thing was the hand painting. I mixed up about six different colors (different hues of greens and browns and grays) using vodka and the Wilton gel colors. They were like watercolors. I speckled the whole head in several hues for a faint mottled look. I painted subtle shades in all the recesses with a fine brush in some of the wrinkles and then a darker color in the ears. I used a tiny brush to paint the eyes with the gel food colors mixed with only a drop or two of vodka.

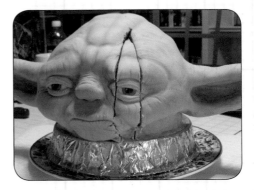

Here are the steps I took to make this Lightning McQueen cake for a friend.

Step 1

I began with 3.25 sheets of chocolate cake, layered with buttercream icing.

Step 2

I found pictures of Lightning McQueen on the internet, printed them, cut them out, and lined the cut image with parchment or wax paper. Cut it out into the shape. I pinned it with toothpicks on the top of the car first and cut around the picture and then repeated for the sides, front, and back. It will help if you have a 3D toy to view as a model.

Step 3

Cut them out and pin them to the cake layers. Then, cut the cake to match the shape. Trim and cut the cake to create the fenders, wheel wells, and spoiler.

Step 4

Crumb coat the cake.

Step 5

Ice the cake.

Step 6

Create fondant accents and designs and add them to the cake just a few hours before delivery. I am so excited I was able to make my own fondant and I had a project to use it on. Just the details are fondant and the red car is buttercream. Hope you enjoy.

Star Wars Cake (Mustafar)

By Michael Angelo Semenchuk

(CementTruck)

(http://www.instructables.com/id/Star-Wars-Cake-Mustafar/)

In a town far, far away, a dad decided to make a *Star Wars* cake for his son's birthday.

Step 1

Bake the cake and make rice crispy treats.

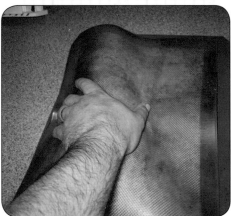

Step 2

Cut a hole in the rice crispy treat hill and add a ramekin (cup).

Step 3

Coat the rice crispy hill in chocolate. Make sure you spread the chocolate to make a flat area of land. You'll see what I mean in a minute. You will also need to pull out the ramekin before you do this step. With a sharp knife, cut jagged pieces of "land" right at the "shoreline" of the rice crispy hill. You can heat the knife to make it cut better.

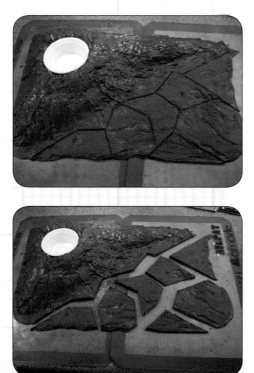

Step 4

Test fit the rice crispy hill on the cake. My cake was a little small, so I had to slice it horizontally, and open it up like a book. Test fit the pieces and trim to fit. Remember where all the pieces went. Use a digital camera for this step.

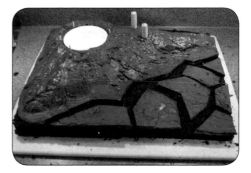

Step 5

Frost the cake. I used super day-glo orange for the frosting. I used an off-the-shelf Pillsbury brand white frosting with a liberal amount of orange food color gel. Top the cake with the hill and the jagged pieces of "land." I microwaved a little of the frosting for ten seconds so it was slightly warm and pourable. I poured it around the area of the ramekin opening, and let it dribble down the side of the hill.

Step 6

Make the sides and added effects. I got the leftover chocolate and re-melted it in the microwave. I poured it over some nonstick surfaces (you can use wax paper) into a large, flat, shape. Once cool, cut it into strips to the height cake. Cut the strips to match the jagged pieces of land and use frosting to stick it to the cake. Melt more chocolate and "weld" the top and side pieces together. For the platform that R2-D2 is standing on, get a sour cream container lid or any lid with some structural relief (little plastic ribs in the structure for interest). Lightly butter or spray some nonstick cooking spray inside the lids. Use these as moulds for melted white chocolate. As an added bonus, I got some blinking lights from the cake decorating section at Wal-Mart. These are supposed to be attached to the stems of champagne glasses, etc. I made a couple of moulds out of a measuring spoon and the center of an apple slicer/corer. I buttered them well and poured more white chocolate in them. Once they started cooling down, I inserted the blinking lights in the white chocolate. Once completely cooled down, I popped them out of the molds and used them on the cake.

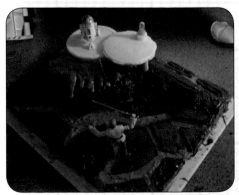

Step 7

If you want, you could add some special effects. The ramekin, which I'm sure you have guessed by now, is for dry ice and water. I'm sure you're kid will enjoy this.

Mach 5 *Speed Racer* Cake

By Tami Chitwood
(tchitwood)
(http://www.instructables.com/
id/How-to-make-a-Mach-5-from-
Speed-Racer-Cake/)

I made this Mach 5 *Speed Racer* cake for my friend's birthday and took some photos along the way because I wanted to share how I made it.

The cake is alternating layers of classic yellow cake and butter pecan cake, with cream cheese icing and chopped walnuts in it in between the layers. It's covered in marshmallow fondant and then hand painted with food colorings. The tires are made from rice cereal marshmallow treats, covered in the fondant, and painted. I also had the car lifted so I could fit in the tires and have it look as if it were really sitting on the tires and not the cake board.

Step 1: Ingredients and Equipment

Here's a list of ingredients and equipment that I used. A lot of the supplies are general cake baking and decorating supplies.

Cake pans for baking the cakes. I used a quarter-sheet pan for both boxes of mix.

- General cake decorating supplies: Mixer, spatulas, turn-table, carving/ clay/fondant tools, mat to roll fondant on*, fondant rolling pin, gel food colors, knife, cake leveler, toothpicks, food-safe paintbrushes, small containers to mix food color "paints" in, 3 quarter-sheet cake boards, X-acto knife, hot glue gun, tape, foil to cover cake boards, etc.

- Ingredients to make cakes and fondant and to mix food colors with. (You will mix the food colorings with something like vodka or clear vanilla extract, not water.)

- A disposable clear plastic container, like the Glad or Reynolds containers, to cut up and use as the windshield.

Here's a link to the alterations made to a box cake mix to make it a little stronger to better support sculpting: http://cakecentral.com/recipes/7445/the-original-wasc-cake-recipe. I used two boxes of cake mix to make this cake. Both were quarter-sheet cakes.

I used store-bought cream cheese icing for this cake instead of making buttercream because the friend the cake was for wanted that type of icing.

There are countless recipes on the Internet that describe how to make the marshmallow fondant, which is pretty yummy, although very sweet! Pre-made fondant can be bought if you do not want to make the marshmallow fondant, but beware that some of the pre-made stuff doesn't taste very appetizing.

Step 2: Bake, Level, Cut, and Stack the Cakes

After baking the cakes as per the recipe, let them cool completely, level off the tops of the cakes as best as you can, and then split/torte each cake into two separate layers (as shown in one of the photos in this step).

Then I stacked the layers, alternating flavors, with a layer of cream cheese icing with walnut pieces sprinkled on, in between the layers. I needed the overall size to be a little longer and thinner so I cut off a side a little bit in and attached it to the end with more icing (as shown in one of the photos in this step). You'll want to have this all on waxed paper and on a cookie sheet for later to make transferring it to the cake boards easier.

While the cakes were cooling, I made the support system of cake boards, which is shown in the next step.

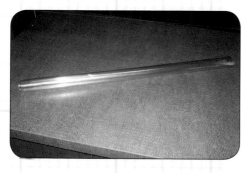

---

*The photos here are of the vinyl mat I use to roll my fondant on. The cake shop I took some classes at suggested this mat for fondant. They sold it there for only $6.00 and it works so great. A lot better than the name-brand mat I had bought before for $20.00.

Step 3: Constructing the Support System/Cake Boards and Cutting General Outline of Cake

I used three 13" × 19" cardboard cake boards for this cake. Two of them were hot glued together and covered in foil, and the third was used to make the support system I came up with.

I drew a general outline/shape of the Mach 5, as if looking down on it from above, on one half of the cake board. Then I cut it out and traced its shape on the other half of the board, cut that out as well, and hot glued them together so it would be sturdier to hold the weight of the cake and the fondant. Kind of like a "footprint" the cake would sit on. I then cut out areas on the sides of this to allow space for the tires later, since this footprint would be at the bottom of the cake.

Then, with the left over scraps, I cut out enough squares and scraps to equal five pillars of cardboard four layers high. I then glued four pieces together to form one pillar and then glued those five pillars to the bottom of the car outline/footprint. I did this a little bit in so they wouldn't easily be seen but still support the cake and allow room for the tires. Then I covered the outline/footprint in foil.

Before connecting the outline piece to the main cake board, I used the outline on the cake as a template of where to cut my basic shape. I laid it on my stacked cakes and cut around it, making it a little bigger than the outline so that the edges of cardboard wouldn't show or jut out from the bottom of the car.

Next, I put a small dab of icing on the bottom of each pillar and positioned the piece, pillar bottoms down, on my large foil-covered cake board that would hold everything, so that the icing would leave a mark where the pillars touched down. I then removed it and cut out the foil in those sections where the icing was on the larger main board so that I could hot glue the pillar/outline support to the main board. I wiped the icing off the bottom of the pillars before gluing it down.

Then I spread a thin layer of icing, without walnuts, on the top of the footprint, flipped it over, and placed it on the cake shape I had cut out. Then, I held the cookie sheet to the bottom and my hand on the top (bottom of the main cake board since it's upside down) and flipped the whole thing, then I lifted the wax paper off the bottom (now top) of the cake.

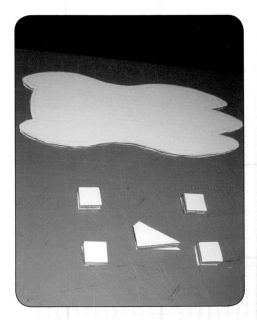

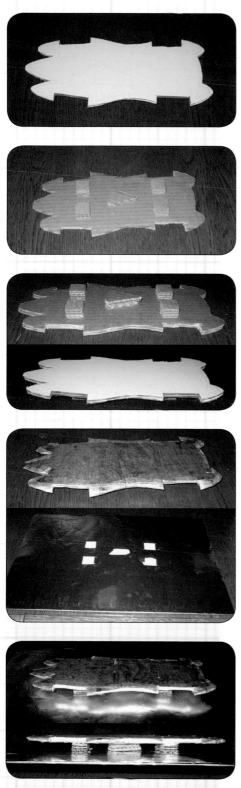

Step 4: Carving the Cake!

Next came the carving of the cake to shape it. I printed lots of reference photos from the internet, many different angles, etc. Then I began carving. I just used a steak knife to carve the cake. I also realized here that I had cut out the wheel area the entire height of the car and shouldn't have, so I used some of the scraps to fill back in the area above the wheel areas with cake and glued them in with the icing. I don't get too detailed here, as it's too hard with cake, so I just got a rough shape. The main details are done in fondant.

Once it's carved to your liking, cover it all in a layer of icing. I use a #45 tip in a piping bag and pipe on the icing so that it's gentle and the cake stays together. Since there are some thin parts, using a spatula to apply it can easily mess up the cake.

Step 5: Applying and Detailing the Fondant

After the carved car is covered in icing, roll out some fondant large enough to cover the car, about the size of the main cake board, so there will be enough to wrap under the car footprint board a little. I rolled out about ⅛" thick, large piece of vinyl that I use for fondant, which it doesn't stick to.

To layer it on the car, I lightly and loosely roll the fondant around my fondant rolling pin to lift it up without its own weight tearing it. Gently lay it, unrolling it from the pin as you go, over the cake. Then use your hands to smooth it all down over the cake and round the parts of the car. You only need to smooth it out over the top of the cab, because you will want to just cut the shape of the cab out in the center to smooth down the fondant because of the seats and dash, etc., which I made out of fondant and then inserted later.

It was a little tricky around the front half of the car. I used my cooking scissors to cut some slits in the fondant in between the cone-shaped areas of the front of the car so I could wrap the fondant down around each cone. Then I cut off the excess around the car, leaving about 1" of fondant at the bottom that I could wrap under.

Next, I used various gum paste tools, and my fingers, to add further details, smoothing it out as best as I could and creating the lines for the doors, trunk/boot, etc. I also formed the rice cereal treats into tire shapes, covered them in fondant, and detailed those as well.

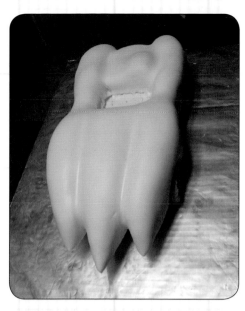

Step 6: Creating the Cab and Final Details

I created the cab items all out of fondant. First I filled in the cab walls and floor with a piece of fondant. Then I made the long rectanglular center part where the stick shifter is and a smaller one for in between the seats. I used a little water on a brush to "glue" them into place. Water on fondant makes it sticky, so it's great to use to stick fondant to fondant. Next came the seats. I formed the bottom part of the seats first, glued them in, then formed the backs of the seats and glued them in place.

Next I painted everything in the cab red with red gel food coloring mixed with a little vodka. You want to use something alcohol based to mix the food colorings with because using water would ruin the fondant. You could use vodka, Everclear, or colorless vanilla extract.

Next came the dash. I formed it with fondant, glued it in place, and put some simple details in like the round dials and the glove box. Then I painted it with the colorings. Next I made the shifter stick from fondant, glued it in and painted it with the edible silver food coloring. I then made the steering wheel out of fondant. I rolled a ball, flattened it and added some basic details, made a simple steering column to put it on, and glued it in place. Then I painted it with the colorings.

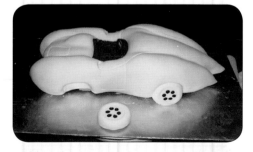

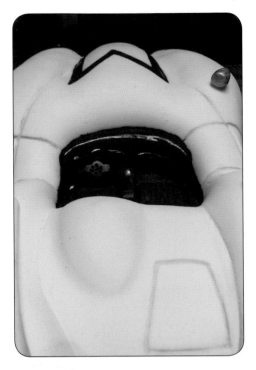

Step 7: Finishing it up!

For the final details, I painted in the doors creases so they would show a little better. Then, I painted the tires and glued them in place with a little water. I made the license plate, glued it in place, and painted on the numbers.

I made oval depressions in the back for the tailpipes, painted them in black, and glued in the tailpipe ends. To make the tailpipes, I rolled tiny little balls of fondant, attached them with water, and used the end of one of my paint brushes to push in the centers. I then painted them. Next I painted the other details of the car: the M on the hood, the number on the doors, etc.

I made the fins out of fondant, with a tooth pick inserted into each one that would help hold it up and secure it to the car, along with a little water. I cut up the plastic container into the windshield shape, a little taller so that I could push it into the cake a little and it would be secure. I set the windshield in place and used it as a template of where to make the curved incision to push the piece down into a little ways.

It's done! My friend loves *Speed Racer* and loved the cake. He knew he was getting a cake but had no idea what it was going to be. Surprises are fun!

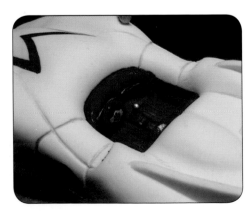

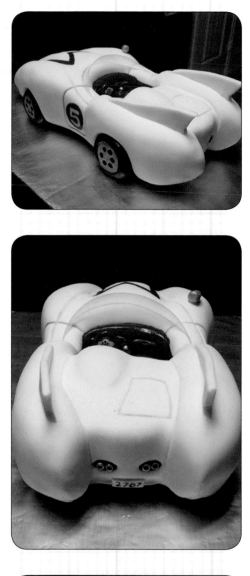

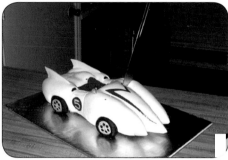

White Chocolate Carriage Cake

By Jennette and Nathan Clark (ndsit)
(http://www.instructables.com/id/White-Chocolate-Carriage-Cake/)

For my cousin's daughter's fourth birthday, I made a white chocolate carriage cake. The carriage is made of white chocolate and sits on a chocolate mud cake. In this Instructable, I'll describe how I made the carriage. I used fondant to create the cobble stone effect. Then I piped in the white to fill in the gaps.

and not the larger one with a soccer ball pattern pressed into it.

- I used the rings that come with the Wilton Ball Pan as the template for the wheels.
- Pink cachous for decorating the carriage. These are the small balls you can get in any baking section of a supermarket.
- You will need piping bags to help pipe the chocolate in places. We made our own, as we needed a smaller hole for most of the work. You may find the chocolate will harden whilst in the piping bag. Just place them in the microwave for–five to ten seconds to soften them up so they can be used again.

Step 2: Making the Bottom Part of the Carriage

First, melt 400 grams of white chocolate buttons in the microwave. I microwave them for thirty seconds. Remove and stir, then repeat until the chocolate is almost completely melted. It is really important to stir the chocolate well each time or the chocolate can burn and you'll have to start again with a fresh packet.

This can also be done in a metal bowl over a pot of boiling water. However, it is vital that the bowl is larger than the pot and that the bowl does not touch the water. It is also very important that you don't get any water at all in the chocolate. I find the microwave method easier and less stressful.

Once the chocolate is melted, pour some into the mold and tilt and twist the mold to make sure the whole thing is covered. Then put it in the fridge to set—use the base ring to ensure the tin is level. Once the chocolate has set, repeat the process above. I did three layers of chocolate to ensure the base was fairly solid and wouldn't break easily.

Step 1: Ingredients and Equipment

- The cake is a chocolate mud cake covered with buttercream and fondant.
- Approximately 1200 grams of white chocolate buttons
- I used the Wilton 16cm Ball Pan as a mold to help create the ball shape of the carriage. Any good cake decorating shop should carry the Wilton range, or you can order one online. Make sure it's the smooth ball

Step 3: Making the Top Part of the Carriage

Pour 400 grams of melted chocolate onto some grease proof paper, and use a plastic spatula to shape a rectangular piece of chocolate that is about 3mm to 5mm thick, 18cm wide, and 25cm long. Wait a few minutes for it to set into a pliable mix. Then cut strips that are about 8mm wide and 25cm long. You will need eight strips in total.

I found it easier to cut through the chocolate into the baking paper underneath, so each strip also had a strip of baking paper attached. Once the strips have all been cut, you may find that they have hardened and that they won't bend without snapping. Just pop them in the microwave for five seconds to soften them up.

Once softened, place the strips in the bowl with the baking paper facing out of the bowl. Once all the strips were placed in the star pattern, I then pushed down in the middle to squash the big lump where they all crossed so it would be a bit smaller. You may need to reheat some of the strips, as they cool while waiting to be placed in the tin.

Once the chocolate has semi-cooled, try to remove the baking paper stuck to the strips. The cooler the chocolate, the easier they are to just peel off. Once completed, place in the fridge to allow them to cool and set hard. Once it has set hard (I left it overnight in the fridge), trim the strips that hung over the edge of the bowl (I used a sharp scalpel). Ensure all strips are flush with the rim of the bowl. This makes it easier to join the two halves together later. I also trimmed and tidied up the sides of the strips to make it look even and tidy—again, use a scalpel to do this.

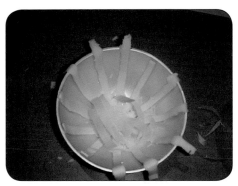

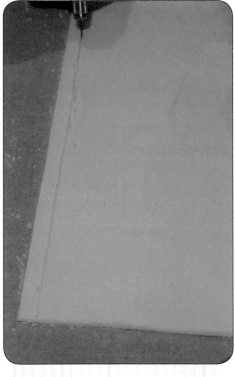

Step 4: Making the Wheels

Using the rings that came with the ball pan, I drew a circle around the inside of them onto some baking paper. They are approximately 80mm in diameter. Then, using a compass, I drew a smaller circle inside with a diameter of 70mm inside of the larger circle. Then, I drew two lines that would be along the N–S and E–W axis of a compass through the middle of the two circles. Next, I drew lines that were along the NE–SW and NW–SE axis of a compass. This star line is the basis of the spokes for the wheels. As we wanted them quite thick, we then measured 2mm on either side of each line and then connected these marks together as shown below.

Now you should have a template of a carriage wheel. Place another sheet of baking paper over this template. If you pipe directly onto the original, the pencil on the paper will mark the chocolate. Melt some more chocolate in

the microwave using the same method as before. This time you will need to place it in a piping bag so you can then pipe the wheel using the template. The thickness of the wheels is up to you, but we made them about 3mm thick. Repeat until you have four wheels.

Step 5: Putting the Two Halves Together

First we made the cake and put it onto the cake board. Then we decorated the cake. Now, using some left over buttercream icing, put a small dollop where the carriage will sit. Make this quite high so the carriage will appear to be off the ground. Place the solid lower half of the ball onto this dollop of buttercream icing.

Before we put the top half on top of this, we removed two strips so that the top appeared to have a doorway on either side. We removed the strips while the lattice was still in the bowl using a scalpel. Next, pipe some melted chocolate around the rim of the lower half ball. Carefully remove the lattice top half and place onto the lower ball before the chocolate piping sets. You will need two people for this.

Then we put small dots of melted chocolate on the strips to hold the pink balls (cachous) in place. Use a pair of wide opening tweezers to make placing the balls easier. The chocolate hardens really quickly so this is also easier is you have one person piping chocolate dots and the other put the cachous on with the tweezers.

To tidy up the top part of the carriage, we attached a small Tinker Bell doll that we had. This hides where the chocolate strips overlapped each other. We were going to add a princess crown, but we thought the Tinker Bell looked cuter.

body, we decorated them as well. We used the side that had been against the paper, as this was the flattest and also the cleanest looking. We just put a blob of melted chocolate into the center of wheel and place the silver and purple balls in this blob.

Once this has set, work out where the wheels will stand against the body, and then put some melted chocolate on the back of the wheels where it touches the body. Also place some melted chocolate where the wheel touches the cake. Place the wheel back in its place and hold it for a few seconds until the melted chocolate has set and holds the wheel on its own.

Repeat for each wheel. As this cake was designed to be viewed from the front, we put all the wheels on with the smooth side towards the front of the cake. If you are making it to be viewed from both sides, then attach the wheels with the smooth side on the outside of both sides of the carriage.

Step 6: Adding the Wheels to the Carriage

Once the main body has been decorated, we need to add the wheels. Before we added the wheels to the

Step 7: Putting It All Together

For the finishing touches, we added some My Little Ponies we borrowed from the birthday girl. We also added some lights to light up the carriage. Then we added some fondant in front of the cake. Then, using the cake letter templates, we added the phrase Happy Birthday. Then the imprint was piped with pink Queen Glitter Writing Gel. Voilà! You then have a finished cake with a white chocolate carriage.

Note: As we finished the cake at 7 a.m. and it had to be delivered at 9.30 a.m. the same day, we were very tired but pleased with the final look of the cake. Everyone loved the cake on the day; the look on the birthday girl's face was priceless and she also received two toy carriages with horses as presents, which was spooky!

Independence Day Surprise Cake

By Steve Quagliotto

(stevequag)

(http://www.instructables.com/id/
Independence-Day-Surprise-Cake/)

I am a math and physics teacher fresh out of college, so with my summers off I enjoy tapping into my creative side and making things for everyone to enjoy. This cake will put your high school geometry skills to use and is sure to be a hit at any summer party. If you are looking for a cake that is both delicious and impressive for your summertime get together, then this is the Instructable for you. This cake is easy but will dazzle your guests by delivering an updated and festive look to a traditional white cake. I start by taking a basic white cake mix and dressing it up with a simple homemade butter crème frosting and some food coloring to please the eyes. Follow my step-by-step instructions and you will be on your way to a show stopper in no time.

Step 1: Ingredients

The ingredients for this cake are very simple and can be found at any local grocery store.

For the Cake

- 2 boxed cake mixes (including the ingredients required to bake them, i.e., eggs, oil, and water)
- Several drops of both red and blue Wilton food colors (I used color gel)
- Crisco or cooking spray (for coating the pan)

For the Buttercream Icing

- 2 sticks of unsalted butter
- 1 pound powdered sugar
- 1 egg white
- 1 or 2 teaspoons vanilla (I like to add the extra teaspoon)
- 1 cup shortening
- 2 tablespoons of milk can be added for extra moisture if necessary. I use shortening for a very white-looking frosting.

Step 2: Making the Cake

Prepare the cake as instructed on the box. It is important you use white cake so that the colors are appropriate for the American flag. (Yes, chocolate is delicious, but this is not the place for chocolate cake.) I used two boxes of cake mix, which yielded 2,000 grams of batter when mixed. The boxes will produce four 8" cake rounds and you will only need three for this cake. Divide the batter into four equal parts (500 grams each if you are using a scale) in bowls large enough to add in color. Mix red into one bowl and blue into another using a few drops or a small amount of food dye gel.

Pour into three greased cake pans and bake as directed. Let cool completely and refrigerate the cake (covered) to make cutting less messy. Use any remaining batter to make delicious cupcakes to snack on while waiting for company!

Step 3: Making the Buttercream Frosting

Yum, nothing is better than a classic buttercream frosting. In a mixer, cream the butter (room temperature) and shortening (or milk if you opt out of using shortening) for about two minutes until light and fluffy. Add in the vanilla and egg white and whip until light and fluffy. Slowly add in the sugar, one cup at a time, until it is incorporated into the butter mixture (5 to 10 minutes).

Note: Buttercream is extremely light and fluffy when at room temperature, which is ideal for stacking and dirty icing the cake.

Step 4: Cutting and Stacking the Cake

Using a cookie sheet (as shown in the pictures) or a fancy cake leveler, make the cakes all uniform in level by shaving off the top of each cake to make them flat and ready for stacking. Cut the red cake in half horizontally so that you have two equal discs. Careful, this can be a little tricky. Take your time and make small cuts, checking to make sure you stay level the whole time. Then do the same thing to the white layer.

Stack the half a red and half a white cake and use a bowl to cut out the center from the cake. Using the same bowl, cut out the center circle of the blue cake (do not destroy it, you will need the outer ring). Place the red/white circle inside of the blue ring. Stack the cakes in the order white, red, blue ring with the white and red in center. Assemble with buttercream between each layer. Crumb coat (coat with a light layer of frosting that acts as the "glue" of the cake) the entire cake and let it set up in the fridge for an hour.

Step 5: Decorate

Now that the cake is set up and hardened, it is time to decorate and make it look pretty. I used a star tip (Wilton #18) to decorate, using a stippling technique, individually pipping each dot of icing. Set aside a small amount of the frosting to color both red and blue. A little less than half of the frosting will need to be white, about a quarter cup will be blue, and the majority will need to be red.

Using a star shaped cookie cutter and different sized bowls (or anything circular), trace out a pattern to follow for decorating your cake. Then have at it! Notice how I saved red for last so that I could just use all remaining frosting when mixing in the food gel colors.

Make sure to have enough frosting (making more is better) before you mix in the colors, so that you don't run out and have to mix and match a new tint of frosting.

Step 6: Enjoy!

The surprise inside this cake is just as exciting as the look of the cake from the outside. Make sure everybody is around when you cut into the cake, and use a very sharp knife to make a perfect cut. I advise you serve this cake cold so that the buttercream is set and won't get messy during cutting (this would make the cake less appealing). If you're not impressed with the look of the outside or inside of the cake, just wait until you taste it. Delicious!

Section 5

Spooky

Making a brain cake is fun, cheap, and great for Halloween parties or get-togethers. This is a basic Instructable to show you how to make the details for this cake; the size and shape depends on your preferences. You can do similar designs for cupcakes or even flat cakes depending on what best fits your needs. This cake is made from two 8" pan cakes that were cut and assembled together to make a more realistic brain cake. The gore is also optional, although it does make the cake look more gruesome and realistic.

Step 1: Ingredients

Here are the basic ingredients that you will need; however, depending on what kind of cake mix or cake recipe you use, it will vary.

- Cake mix with necessary ingredients (follow the instructions on your recipe or box)
- Frosting (we bought ours, but feel free to mix your own)
- Mini marshmallows (a whole package preferably)
- Powdered sugar
- Cake dye, especially the colors green and red
- Oil (to grease your hands with later)

Step 2: Mix and Bake the Cake

Follow the directions on your box/recipe and mix together the cake. We separated ours into two 8" round pans for this cake, but you can make any size or shape you want. A good tip is to place the bottom of the pan on parchment paper, draw out the shape of it, and then cut it out. Grease the pan as usual and place the parchment cut out on the bottom of the pan. Then grease the paper and pour the cake batter over it. Basically this guarantees that the cake will come out of the pan much more easily than normal. Cut the cake to shape and cover it with a layer of frosting. The frosting will act as a glue and will hold the fondant onto the cake.

Step 3: Melt Marshmallows

Now that the cake is done, it's time to make the fondant. If you have fondant mix, you can use that instead of making your own, or you can buy fondant from stores like Joann's. My marshmallow fondant is completely edible and basically tastes like super sweet marshmallow taffy. Place a large amount of marshmallows into a microwavable bowl. (You will need a lot more than this for a large cake, I am just making a sample here.) *Lightly* sprinkle the marshmallows with water. Please do not add too much water. You only want to lightly moisten the marshmallows with a little water so that they cook better. Melt the marshmallows in the microwave. I would put them in for thirty seconds, stir, and then place them in for another thirty seconds to completely melt them.

Step 4: Make the Fondant

Okay, this is kind of difficult and involved, but if you have ever made bread, you might be familiar with some of the steps here. First, sift the powdered sugar onto a large board and make a mound in the center. You really need to sift this stuff—it looks super fluffy, but it has a lot of little clumps that you normally do not notice. These clumps are a major problem when making fondant because they make it bumpy and uneven.

Oil your hands with the cooking oil of your choice (you could also use butter, Crisco, or any type of grease for this job). Basically, you are greasing your hands so that the sticky marshmallows do not stick to you. Get a friend to scrape the melted marshmallows onto the mound of sugar, then dump a lot of powdered sugar on top of it. It should be completely covered. Gently knead in the sugar until it gets a thicker consistency. Make sure you keep it well covered in sugar and keep your hands well greased. Once it is thick enough to not run all over the place, knead it much harder as you would for bread dough. Basically, to knead you use the bottom of your palms to push the dough forward and then use your fingers to pull it back to center. Do this over and over again, applying more sugar as it soaks it all up. When the sugar dough turns to the consistency of soft taffy, then it is done.

Step 5: Color and Shape Fondant

Separate your fondant into small tennis ball shapes and then rip them open with your fingers. Add equal parts of green and pink to make a realistic brain color. Knead and mix the fondant until the colors evenly mix and are fully incorporated. You can also make some piles have more pink than green and others grayer and darker. Roll the fondant into thin strips of various lengths and thicknesses.

oblong ball shape and is placed on the lower half of one side of the cake. There will be small areas of white frosting in between the layers—this can optionally be covered with fake blood.

Step 6: Place the Fondant on the Cake

Carefully place the fondant strips one at a time onto the cake. Start with one end and then swirl the rest of the length around to create S and G shapes. Each length of fondant will create a little cluster of brain. Add the next length right next to the cluster you have created and use the same technique to make more clusters. Do this until the entire cake is covered in clusters. You can also add a brain stem, which is an

Step 7: Fake Blood

Add dark corn syrup with red dye to create a blood mixture. The pictures show the right color the fake blood should look. If you can only find clear corn syrup, add some blue or purple to create a darker color. You will need a lot more of this to cover a whole cake. Also you can add flavorings to this mixture if you like. Use a spoon or butter knife to drip the blood into the cracks so that you can cover the white frosting up. You can also spread it onto the plate to give the cake a very gory appearance. I stuck in some knives to make it look more scary.

Animated Halloween Cake

By Will Turnbow

(Nannuu)

(http://www.instructables.com/
id/Animated-Halloween-Cake/)

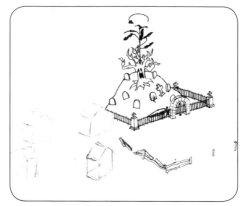

Create an animated Halloween cake using fondant, motors, cardboard, wire, toys, clay, Styrofoam, glue, paper, metal, lights—you name it. This one we made for our daughter's second birthday since it is close to Halloween. There are so many Halloween ideas out there. I made the mistake of looking online to see what people make for their Halloween decorations. Wow, so many great ideas out there. Took me a week of reading about other projects to finally give up and go back to our cake.

Step 1: Planning

Be sure to attempt to sketch out what you want in the end. I find this most helpful to find flaws in my own plans, and it also makes it easier to explain to anyone who volunteers to help me.

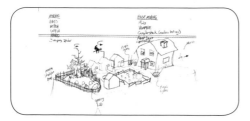

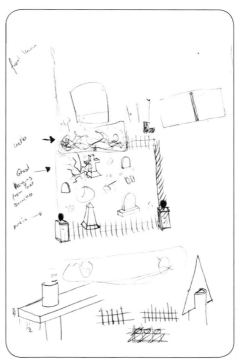

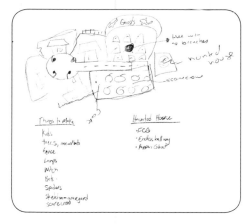

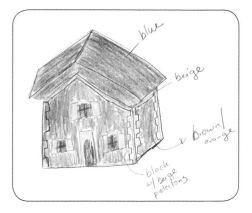

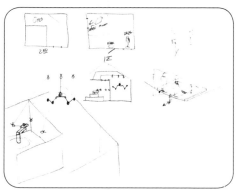

Step 2: Flying Crank Pepper's Ghost

The best part of the cake is the Flying Crank Pepper's Ghost in the haunted house window. The worst part of the cake, no one could see the awesome ghost in the window due to my bad design. Not many people were tall enough to lean over the cake to see in the window, and those that were tall enough were too shy to do so. Doh! Ah, next time.

I have to give credit to the FCG's creator Doug Ferguson. I've also included the Pepper's Ghost effect to this. It's the same effect the Haunted Mansion uses at Disneyland. So if you want to ruin your vacation to Disney, look it up. The most difficult part of the FCG was finding a material that was light enough to bend on such a tiny ghost. I never did find one, but I think the outcome was good enough. I tried shredded paper mache, feathers, and a few materials. I finally settled on one white material that was the most heavy but still flexible. It didn't allow the elbows to bend like the other stuff but overall it looked better. We ended up adding fishing weights to the arms to pull them down when the string had slack. They could not be seen in the end product.

The motor runs at 12 rpm, which is a bit faster than I wanted but all I had to use. Gearing it added too much work.

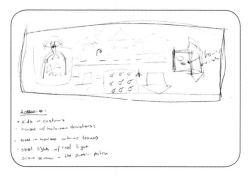

117

Once it was buried in the house, you couldn't hear it at all. The reflective glass is a trimmed CD case slitted into the foam core. I added a toy makeup desk behind the plastic so that the ghost had something to appear before. The green light fades in and out to make the ghost appear and disappear.

Step 3: Jumping Spider

I also really like the jumping spider on the pumpkin. Very easy really. A 3 rpm motor with a spring piece of metal rotates below. The spider has a wire (rod) going down through the cake that lines up with the springy metal. There is a bracket that blocks the springy metal as the motor rotates toward the rod. Once the motor goes so far, the spring finally pops off of the bracket and pops the spider's rod, which shoots him up. So he jumps about every twenty seconds. In my haste, I didn't get a picture of the underside of this mechanism, despite hours of testing to make sure the jump was perfect.

Step 4: Miscellaneous Movements and Lights

I was able to recycle the dual mechanism I'd made for a previous cake to use on the moving tombstone and skeletal arm coming out of the ground. Just a little adjustment and voilà! The only bad thing is that, the day before, we added the fondant to the floor and the runny sugar ran down into the shaft that was pushing the tombstone stopping it. If you ever need to cement anything, use some raw glucose, holy cow. Took about a half hour to clean that all up and get it running again. Whew, I thought it was a gonner at first.

The motors strip out so easily. The coffin was really easy. Just use a 30 rpm motor with an arm on it, add the shaft, and add the skeleton arm. It took longer to make/size/cut/glue a pattern for the coffin. I refused to buy one even though you can easily find miniature coffins around. I had to add a quarter to the underside of the lid to keep it pulling down to the hand. More fun to make than buy. The bats and ghosts are just hooked straight to shafts that are hooked to motors. These were taken from kids Halloween rings. Very easy. It was more difficult to run the shaft up the tree, but we got it no problem. Lili molded the witch flying around the middle house. Turned out really cute I thought. Again, it was hooked directly to a motor below the cake.

The tree was originally going to be a Lemax spooky tree, but it wasn't nearly big enough for what we wanted so we molded our own using Sculpy. Just wish I had thought of that ahead of time and added some glowing eyes. I did not have any tiny LEDs around the night we made that decision. Yep, I need to stock up on more junk, just in case. Franky, Drac, and the Mummy were picked up as a set at the dollar store, score! Franky and Dracula move from a piece of wood moving back and forth below the haunted house. The door opens via string attached as well and closes due to an elastic strap behind the hinge. This was one of the worst ideas on the cake. There were better ways to do this, but I wanted to try an easier way, which turned out much less effective (and locked up halfway through the party). I even had some nice rollers I could have used that I didn't even think about. Never again, I say! We added the Mummy to a separate room using only an adjustable LED strobe kit. We used the coffin template from the graveyard for this coffin as well. Easy as can be.

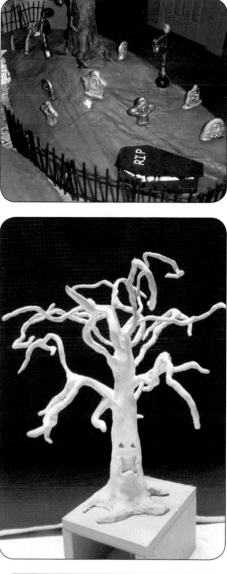

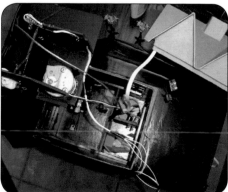

Step 5: More Miscellaneous Junk

The four houses were baked with Wiltons house pan. It makes a decent base for a house. We wanted them to all look different. Lots of colored fondant. The pumpkin patch is sunk so that we could add a chocolate cake here. We were hoping to hide a cake there so the entire ground looked the same. So, all of the ground is fondant. We also covered the haunted house with fondant to keep continuity with the other houses. The goal was to be a bit spookier, but we really ran out of time the night before the party. By the way, the ground you see around the yard of the haunted house took two of us about two and a half hours to make. Never thought it would take that long.

The bushes that hide the purple lights are made from a sponge and painted to look like fall bushes. The hills that the graveyard and haunted house sit on are foam used for walls. I glued together sheets of foam, then cut them with the band saw, and finally formed them with a knife and sandpaper. Lili made all of the gravestones from clay. I used the scrap from this Styrofoam to make the pillars for the gargoyles. The small trees and pumpkins were also made from clay. Most of stuff we made, but we did cheat this time and bought some Lemax miniature stuff for lighting the streets around the town

and the fence around the pumpkin patch and gargoyles (we made the pillars).

The kids are actually Polly Pockets with their legs cut off to shorten them. Then Lili made costumes for each child for the Halloween celebration. With so much other junk to do for this party, it really made it easier to buy some of the accessories (we decorated the yard as well). The skeleton in the coffin was ripped off of a Halloween straw. I think everything else we made on the cake; there was still a lot to do, really. Crushed dreams. I really wanted to light a piece of frosted plexi/lexan above and to the right of the haunted house to look like a moon. To me that would have finished the cake. Was not to be, time ran out. I also wanted some chasing ghosts using a light and rotating disc (with ghost images cut in) coming from the haunted window against some mesh. That one did not make it either, but that is okay—I do not know how good that would look at a small scale anyway. Also some fog in the graveyard would have been cool. We tried fog from dry ice and it goofed the fondant to a sticky mess. Must find a way around that next time. There is about 12 pounds of fondant total on the cake. Most of it went uneaten, but we wanted it all to look the same.

Sculpted Zombie Cake

By Tami Chitwood

(tchitwood)

(http://www.instructables.com/
id/How-to-make-a-sculpted-
zombie-cake/)

This is my Instructable on how to make a sculpted zombie cake. I made this cake for a very good friend, who is a huge horror and comic fan, for his October birthday. This was made custom to look like him, but you could tailor the look how you please. It was a surprise for him and he absolutely loved it.

Depending on your artistic skill, this could be hard or easy. I'm an artist, new to cake decorating, and this is my fourth sculpted cake (self-taught). Total time spent on it from the start of baking to completion was about 12 hours over the course of three days. On one day, I baked all the cakes and froze them. The next day, I made the tombstone and the final day I made the zombie and finished it up.

The tombstone is red velvet cake covered in fondant. The zombie is red velvet cake covered in fondant. The fingers are all fondant and the grass/ground is fondant. The dirt is made from chocolate sandwich cookies (minus their cream layer) and ginger snaps ground up in the food processor. It was hand painted with gel food colorings mixed like watercolors (but not with water).

Step 1: Ingredients and Equipment

Here's a list of supplies that I used. There are also the recipes or links I used. A lot of the supplies are general cake baking and decorating supplies.

- Cake pans for baking the cakes. I used a quarter-sheet pan for the tombstone and two 8" rounds and two 6" rounds for the zombie.
- General cake decorating supplies: Mixer, spatulas, turn-table, carving/clay/fondant tools, matt to roll fondant on, fondant rolling pin, gel food colors, knife, cake leveler, toothpicks, food-safe paintbrushes,

small containers to mix food color "paints" in, three-quarter-sheet cake boards, X-acto knife, hot glue gun, tape, cake support dowels, foil to cover cake boards, etc.

- Ingredients to make cakes, buttercream icing and fondant and to mix food colors with. (You will mix the food colorings with something like vodka or clear vanilla extract, not water.)

Here's the link to the alterations made to a box cake mix to make it a little stronger to better support sculpting: http://cakecentral.com/recipes/7445/the-original-wasc-cake-recipe. I used three boxes of cake mix to make this cake. One for the quarter sheet, one for the two 8" rounds, and one for the two 6" rounds.

There are dozens of recipes online that describe how to make marshmallow fondant, which is pretty yummy, although very sweet! Pre-made fondant can be bought if you do not want to make the marshmallow fondant, but beware that some of the pre-made stuff doesn't taste very appetizing.

Buttercream Icing

Here's a simple recipe for the buttercream icing, a 2-pound batch. This uses shortening in place of butter. I'm in Texas and butter doesn't hold up as well right now. If you don't have a stand mixer or don't want to make your own icing, you can buy some pre-made.

- 2 cups shortening
- 2 pound bag powdered cane sugar (or approximately 8 cups)
- 4 tablespoons meringue powder
- 2 teaspoon vanilla extract (use clear vanilla if you want your icing to be white)
- 2 teaspoon butter flavor (use clear flavor if you want your icing to be white)
- 1 teaspoon almond extract
- Water

Directions

- Sift together powdered sugar and meringue powder into large bowl. Set aside.
- Mix the flavor extracts together in a measuring cup. Add enough water to the mixture to bring the amount to ½ cup. Put this into a mixer bowl with the shortening.
- Add about ¼ of the sifted powdered sugar/meringue powder mixture to the shortening and flavors in the mixer bowl. Beat on a slow speed with the paddle beater, and then slowly incorporate the rest of the powdered sugar mix into the mixer bowl as it's slowly mixing. Once it's all in there, I usually turn it up a notch in speed for about 1.5 to 2 minutes. Then it's done!
- Keep it covered until you are ready to use it, as it will "crust" over if you are leave it uncovered to the air for too long.

Step 2: Bake All Your Cakes!

Let them cool completely after baking, then level the cake tops. Once they are cooled, put them in the freezer while you build the support system for the tombstone (next step). I wrap mine all separately in plastic wrap and put them in the freezer.

Step 3: Building the Tombstone Support and Cake Board

This was my first time making a cake with a tall thin structure like the tombstone and, because I wanted it to be cake, I had to do some brainstorming to find a way to make it work. First, I hot glued two quarter-sheet cake boards together to create a thicker over-cake base.

Then, on the third cake board, I measured out the size of the actual quarter-sheet pan, plus extra for a corner stand, and cut it out. I scored and bent this piece at the end of the sheet cake size to form a flap. This flap became its base/stand bottom that was glued to the corner of the cake board and trimmed flush with the main cake board.

I then decided on a slight angle so that the cake of the tombstone would very slightly lean back. I used dowels to support the back of the tombstone board. To make it more stable, I marked out where the bottom of the two dowels would hit the cake board, tracing around them to get the right size marks on the board. Then I cut out the little holes with an X-acto blade all the way through all three layers of cake board that is in this area. I squeezed hot glue into one of the holes and inserted the dowel straight up and pushed it all the way down and then repeated with the other dowel.

Next I leaned back the vertical part of the tombstone board until it hit the dowels. I put hot glue where they met and then put a little tape over each to secure it until the hot glue was dry. Then I covered it in the cake foil.

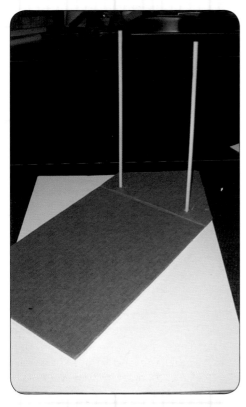

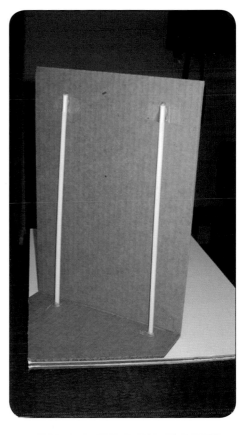

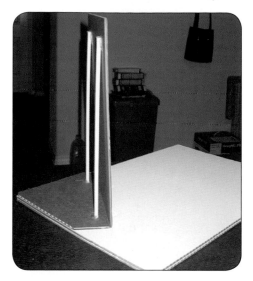

cake into tall skinny pieces and layered them up the vertical tombstone board, with buttercream in between the layers. I pushed two dowel supports into the cake surface to give it some more support. Then I covered it in a buttercream crumb coat. This is done to give the fondant a surface it can stick to and to help seal in the moistness of the cake so it won't dry out. I used a piping tip and bag and just piped it on, because the cake was a little crumbly cut like this, but it's fine to spatula it on.

Next, roll out white fondant large enough to cover the front, top, and sides, with a few inches extra to wrap around the cake board backing a few inches. Since the back of the tombstone is the cake board and support system, I didn't completely cover the back. Now here's where you make your tombstone however you like. You can use a food-safe brush to brush on water to attach fondant to fondant, so I did that here with all the details.

Once it's done, it's time to paint it. Water makes fondant sticky (which is why it's good to use to stick fondant to fondant); but you don't want your fondant getting ruined when you paint it, so you use an alcohol-based mixer, like vodka or clear vanilla extract. It won't ruin the fondant, and it evaporates fast and leaves the color behind. I mixed up a watery gray and gave it a wash (then added some mossy green areas later at the end because I decided it needed some).

Step 4: Building the Tombstone

Once the base is done, take the sheet cake out of the freezer and get your buttercream ready. I sliced up the

Step 5: Add Some Grass/ Ground to the Main Cake Board Base

Roll out enough green fondant to cover the cake board. Spread a thin layer of buttercream on the board surface so the fondant will stick. Cover it with fondant and remove an area of fondant where the zombie will go. I gave this green fondant and simple crosshatch grassy-type texture.

Later, after the zombie was in place, I then used more green fondant to build a ridge around the zombie that was raised, up to the edge of the tombstone, that would help hold in the "dirt" and make it look like the ground was being pushed out. I also gave this the same texture.

Step 6: Build Your Zombie

Take your two 8" rounds and two 6" rounds out of the freezer and stack them in this order, with buttercream between layers: 8" on bottom, second 8", then a 6", and the second 6" on top. Next, take a knife and carve your basic zombie's shape, whatever or whoever that may be. I gave mine the basic shape then carved out a few details, like depressions where I would add the eyes in later and basic mouth, nose, and ear creases.

Once you have it carved, give it a crumb coat of buttercream. I just used a cake spatula on this part. Next, roll out enough white fondant to cover this. I smoothed out the fondant, using first my fingers and then my tools to further define the shapes of the facial features. The eyes and the ears were added after this.

On the eye that's there, I added the eye (a smooth, slightly domed circle) and then the eyelids over top and added detail (and gave it that nice milky zombie eye look when painting). On the missing eye, it is actually inset a bit so there's a hollow where the eye used to be. I created a deeper depression with my thumb and then added the eyelids.

I formed the shape of the ears and detailed them after I connected them. Then, I went to town with the details of the sagging, rotting skin and his hair and facial hair. I formed the fingers out of fondant. I then hand painted him. I mixed up nine different hues of different colors and some more that were "watery" than others.

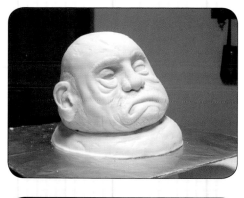

Step 7: Putting It All Together

Once the zombie is finished, spread some buttercream on the cake board in the area you left for him and set him in place. Now is when I added the grass ridge. I then added the fingers coming over the ridge.

The final step is adding in your "dirt" of ground up chocolate sandwich cookies and ginger snaps. I filled in the area within the ridge, with a little spilling over for effect, piling up some around his fingers and even putting some in and on top of his ears and on top of his head.

And now frighten, butcher, and enjoy!

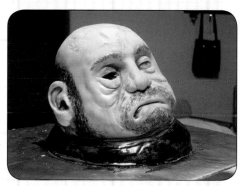

The Witch's Kitchen Cake

By Dee Dee Pierce
(ddpie)
(http://www.instructables.com/
id/The-Witchs-Kitchen-Cake/)

This spooky Halloween cake may look diabolical, but I can assure you, it tasted heavenly. The entire display is made of various sugar art techniques and recipes or other food products and is completely edible except for a couple of items used for supports and, of course, the lighting. It sits on a custom wooden base that measures 18" × 18" and the witch measures about 12" tall. The cauldron is chocolate cake with chocolate buttercream icing and the tree trunk is yellow cake with maple buttercream icing.

Let me start by saying, I'm not a professional pastry chef, nor have I had any culinary training. I just happen to love sugar art as a hobby! Because I like to try to do things I haven't seen before (or try to improve upon what I've seen), I learn through trial and error. This cake was no exception! I'll share with you each component of the project and what I think would work better next time. I've included as many details as I possibly can for those who are interested in learning more about the actual sculpting of the witch and execution of the construction process for this cake. I hope that it helps.

That said, this certainly isn't a project for a beginner. You'll need to have worked with fondant and gum paste and, of course, be able to bake a cake. If you need help learning to make and/or work with fondant, there

are many resources on the Internet. In addition, you'll have to be comfortable with using power tools to build the base, or else just have someone build it for you. I did all of the work myself, with the exception of the actual cake assembly. You'll definitely need an extra set of hands for the last steps.

- 4" × ½" finished boards of inexpensive light weight wood (I used aspen pine)
- Velcro (even if you get self adhesive, you'll need to glue it or staple it)
- Wood glue
- Duct tape
- Electrical tape
- Nails
- Screws
- ¾" PVC pipe
- 3 flanges
- 1 small string of battery-operated LED lights (for the witch's eyes)
- 1 small string of Christmas lights (I used electric because the battery-operated ones I had were not bright enough)
- Gift wrap or cake board wrap
- Drill
- Miter saw
- Table saw or router (only if you want a removable bottom, but this isn't really necessary)

I started with an 18" × 18" × ¾" MDF board for the top. Next, I used 4" × ½" aspen pine boards for the base that would house the extra lighting and switch. I used a table saw to cut a groove along the boards, so that later I could add a ¼" thick bottom that I would be able to remove completely if and when I needed to work on the electrical wiring. Next, using a miter saw, I mitered the ends of the aspen board to form a box that measured 13" × 13" and set in with about 2" all the way around. That way, when it was finished (and turned over), I would have room to hold the sides and safely move the cake stand. I glued three sides of the "box" to the bottom with wood glue and, when dry, turned it over and secured them with small finishing nails.

For the "access" panel and for added support, I glued a brace piece across the open end. Then I glued pieces of Velcro on the support piece as well as

Step 1: Building the Cake Board Base

First off, have a well thought out plan. I had a pretty good idea of where everything was going to be placed, how big the cakes were going to be, and how the lighting would work in the cake. In addition, I built this base/cake stand with the intention of using it for a couple of future projects. My "tree hugging" daughter will be glad to hear that I was recycling and/or already had on hand almost everything I used. (Exactly how many strands of Christmas lights does one really need to have on hand?) The only thing I had to buy was the PVC pipe and flanges.

You will need:

- 1 MDF or other wood board, cut to size and at least ¾" thick (really, these cakes were heavy!)

the access panel. You'll want to dry fit this first to make sure that your access panel will shut completely and securely. In hind sight, I would have moved the brace support inward and put blocks on each side for the Velcro contacts. Even without a bottom, there wasn't much room for my hands to fit underneath to make adjustments after the cake was assembled.

Next, I turned the stand over, upright. I marked where the witch and the cauldron would be placed. At this point, I already had the witch completed and I knew that my cauldron cake would be at least 9" in diameter and would be at least 5" to 6" tall from the base of the coal lights (that's without the candy top). For both the witch and the cauldron, I used ¾" PVC pipe and plastic plumbing flanges for the supports. Then I drilled holes in the cake board, using a ⁹⁄₁₆" hole drill bit, where the wires would be threaded through the pipes. I made two smaller holes, using a regular large drill bit for the pumpkin lights. Where the cake base (flange) would sit, I drilled four holes in conjunction with the holes on the flange. The holes were just big enough to hold two orange lights each for the lighting of the fiery coals (okay, that wasn't pre-planned, just lucky). Sorry that I didn't get a photo of the top side pre-drilled, but I do have pictures of the lighting in the next step.

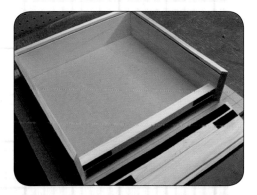

Step 2: Adding the Lighting to the Cake Base

I painted the pedestal base black with acrylic craft paint and, when dry, covered the bare top of the MDF board with a double layer of gift wrap. Then I pre-drilled two holes in each flange (one for the witch, one for the cauldron) so that they could be screwed to the board.

Next, I punched out the paper where the holes were for the cauldron base and screwed it into the base board. I measured and used the miter saw to cut the PVC pipe for the cake to about 5.5". I fed the end of the light strand (that would light up the green goo on the cauldron) up through the pipe from underneath. My light string had a plug on one end and a receptacle on the other. So, I cut off the receptacle end and taped the wires individually with electrical tape. Of course, ideally, you would want to use a strand that ended with one light and not a receptacle. I just happened to use what I had on hand.

As for the color of the lights, you will have to make some decisions according to your cake design. My candy top was clear but tinted green; I had made this ahead of time to test out the recipe. Originally, I thought I would use green lights for the top and orange lights for the bottom coals. But it turned out that it looked much better and brighter with the white lights when I did a little test run. I ended up using about ten white lights for the top and eight orange lights for the bottom. This worked out perfectly and gave just enough light for the effects I was looking for. Originally, I was going to use two battery-operated strands that I had, but when I did a test run with the candy piece and set the lights underneath it on a plate, the lights weren't strong enough at all.

Because I changed my mind and went with the electrical strand, I then had to go back and drill a hole in the access panel just small enough for the cord to fit through, so that it would sit level on the table. I think it's important to point out that, when I designed the box, I was sure to place the access panel on the "back" side of the display.

The last step was to add some protection for the candy coal lights as well as something that would lift the cauldron cake up off the cake board. I ended up using an acrylic food canister container that I had because it happened to fit perfectly over the flange. I had to cut it down to size though, so I put a piece of masking tape all the way around and marked where I wanted to cut. I used a hand saw, cut through all the way around, and then lightly sanded the edge. Next, I drilled a ¾" hole so that the pipe would fit through the center. Now I had something for my cake to sit on that would also protect the lights from touching the cake or candy coals.

Now, give your lighting a test run to be sure that everything is working. Also, in the photo, I show the light string hanging out; but before the actual cake assembly, I pushed those wires back through the pipe so that, when I put the cake on, it would touch the wires and they'd be protected.

Step 3: Making the Witch's Frame and Wiring the Eyes

I knew that the cauldron would be a three-layer cake and planned on it being about 5" to 6" tall (that's not including the coals). So I planned my witch accordingly and made her to be about 12" tall in total. Although I plan on saving her, I still wanted to make her technically "edible" (that's part of the challenge, right?). This meant not having any wiring touching any of the edible portions.

I used a small string of battery-operated Christmas LED lights for her eyes. I took a bendable soda straw, cutting off at least half of the long end, and a small portion of the short end. This way, I'd be able to bend it into position right before sculpting. Next, I threaded two of the red lights up through the end. Later, I would secure them in place with white electrical tape so that they wouldn't move during the sculpting.

For her body support, I cut another piece of PVC pipe to about 10" (sorry, I didn't measure, I guestimated). Of course, our torch was out of propane, so I just used a candle and heated up the middle where her waist would be bent. (I wanted her hunched over). I did this a little at a time, heating then bending, until I got what was just a little less than a 30° angle. (Just eyeball it.) Then I gave it a good roughing up with some coarse sandpaper. This gave the pipe some "tooth" so that the food products I used would stick to it and not slide down the pole. I washed it really well with soap and water.

Next, I drilled a hole straight through where her arms would go. As you can see, I used soda straws again, only, this time, I fitted them together and utilized the bendable portion of the straws for her joints. I tried to get close to anatomical proportions but left them just a bit longer, knowing that once I sculpted the body I could just cut them shorter if and when needed. I also made sure that the piece that went through the pipe went all the way through and that the other straw fit all the way into that one. Even still, I left myself a little bit of playing room in case I needed to make her shoulders narrower or wider when I started sculpting.

After placing the arms in, I took the "eyeball" straw and stuck it up through the pipe and behind the arm straws. I placed the PVC frame into the third flange and screwed it to the board so it would only serve as a stand. I had to cut the bottom of the wires so that, when I went to put her on the cake board, all I had to do was feed the wire down through the pre-drilled hole on the board. Now that the "work" was done, it was time to have some fun and sculpt the witch!

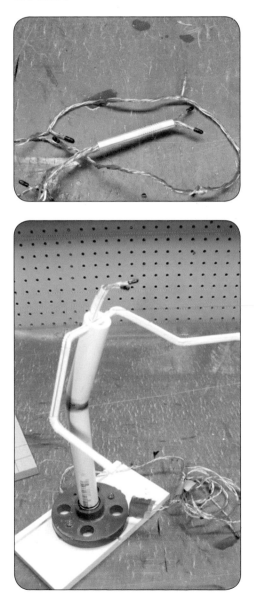

Step 4: Sculpting the Witch's Body and Head Base

I've sculpted fondant figures before, but never a size this big. I did know that fondant, when soft, is difficult to sculpt without disfiguring your figure. So I had planned on using Rice Krispie Treats as a base form so that I could let that harden and have it serve as a solid foundation for the fondant covering. I used the recipe on the box but left out the butter.

Rice Krispie Treat Base

- 5 oz mini marshmallows
- 3 cups Rice Krispies Cereal

Pour marshmallows into a large bowl, microwave for about 2 minutes, and then stir. Continue to microwave at 30-second intervals until completely melted. Quickly stir in the cereal. Working with this stuff can be a nightmare, so here are a few tips:

- Place the mixture into a glass bowl and set it on a heating pad that has been covered with a towel. Cover the bowl with plastic wrap then cover that with part of your towel. Set the heating pad to the lowest setting. This will keep your mixture from drying out and also keep it warm and pliable, giving you more time to sculpt with it.
- Rub a little bit of shortening on your hands and fingers and/or a little bit of water. This will allow you to handle it and get it stuck to the pipe without it sticking to you.
- Start from the bottom and work your way up. I did a cone shape for the dress, then went all the way up the pipe just past the shoulders. Then I went back and added more here and there to get her shape. You'll want to really pack in the cereal, so that you have a pretty solid form. If needed, you can use a paring knife or a pumpkin saw to carve in more details of the shape after it has hardened.
- Be sure to exaggerate whatever shape you want because you'll be covering it with thick fondant and you'll lose some of your "curves." For instance, I knew that I wanted a "hunch back" for aesthetic reasons but also in order for the cape to go flowing off of her back. I also had planned for her to have a hood, so I exaggerated the hump. This helped hold her hood up when I got to that step. Her "butt" I did for similar reasons. It allowed the bottom of the cape to rest on it, keeping it away from her body, thus giving her more dimension.

Okay, so the body was looking good. Next, it was time to move onto the head and neck. I used my personal favorite, MMF (marshmallow fondant), and tinted it with a neon green food coloring. You can use store bought; however, it is much cheaper to make your own. I really don't want to go into particulars here on how to work with fondant or make it (this tutorial is more about the cake construction), but you can find resources online easily.

So, first I taped the eye lights with white electrical tape, bending and shaping them into place. Then I taped them more securely to the straw. I started with only a small ball of fondant, shaping it around the eyes. I built on that, using smaller torn pieces of fondant. Similar to how you see people creating head busts out of clay. This step only serves as a base for the rest of the head and face, so just worry about the general shape.

Next, I shaped the neck and smoothed that down over the tops of the shoulders. I let the whole piece dry and harden over night before moving on to the next step.

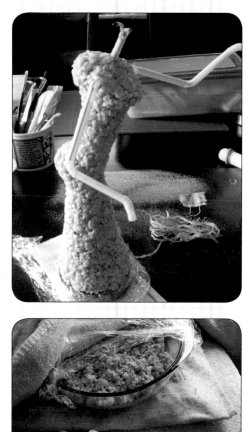

Step 5: Sculpting the Fondant Witch

I began by adding more onto her head and then, again, exaggerated some of the areas that would later be her main features (think bone structure). So I concentrated on the eyebrow bones

first, then pinched her nose, and then sculpted her chin.

Next, it was a matter of pushing and shaping her cheeks using my fingers and thumbs. When I got her basic face shape, I used a fondant tool to add in the details, like her nostrils and her lips. Then I gave more shape to her eyes and more detail there. I also added little rolls of white fondant for the whites of her eyes, which served to be more of an anchor for the LED lights. Using the fondant tool, I carved in some wrinkles around her mouth, eyes, and forehead.

Once I was satisfied with the shape of her face, I used gel food coloring to hand paint her eyebrows, gave her some eyeliner, and what's a witch without the black mole? So I stuck on a little ball of fondant and painted that black too. Then I used a moss green food coloring powder (also known as "petal dust") for the shading and a bright yellow for her cheek bones.

So now, it was time to get her dressed. I used black MMF, covered her bodice, and also made rolls and stuck them vertically on her skirt. This would help create the ruffles in her skirt later. Then I rolled out fondant, about ¼" thick, cut it, and draped it over as a skirt. I made the twisted belt and attached that. Tip: When dressing your figure, cut out the clothing pieces as if they were pieces of a dress pattern. Then "dress" or apply them from the inside closest to the body outward.

Next, I started covering her arms with the green fondant. As you can see in one of the photos, I removed her "pinching hand" and stuck it into a Styrofoam block to dry so that the fingers would hold their shape. Also, fondant gets pretty heavy; in fact, when I went to attach that arm, I ended up inserting a wire through the straw for added support. Plus, I made her a little temporary crutch to hold her arm up while it dried. The other arm went on much more smoothly because she had a walking stick for support. I made the stick first, letting it dry over night so that it would be hard. Also, this arm would be closer to her body, so I didn't have to worry so much about the weight. I stuck it right to her bodice, then, after shaping her hand and forearm, rested them on the walking stick.

After the arms, sleeves, and hands were in place, secured, and dried, it was time to add the cape. I used a fondant rolling pin with guide bands to roll out more fondant, this time making it only about ¼" thick. I cut it slightly smaller at the top, leaving it wider at the bottom. I pinched in some folds at the top, then attached the top around her neck using an artist brush dampened with water. Next I did the hood, tucking it under and shaping it as I went.

A little touch up paint here and there and, of course, I also had to polish her "fingernails" with black. I wired her battery pack back on just to check her eye lights (not that it would have done me any good at this point if they didn't work, I just wanted to see how she looked).

At this point she was done, except for her hair. I waited several days for the fondant to dry and harden before attempting to add it. Even then, you'll have to be careful because even when dried, fondant is fragile and can crack, crumble, and/or break on you.

One last tip: If your Rice Krispie Treat base is too bumpy, it will show through the fondant. You can use regular icing as "putty" and smooth over all of the cracks. Just attach the fondant right after doing this so that the icing is still wet and the fondant will stick to it.

Total time it took for constructing the witch was about three days, with an additional week of drying time before the actual cake construction.

Step 6: Making the Fondant Pumpkins

The witch was done and, while I waited for her to dry, I worked on the pumpkins. They were actually quite easy to make, it was handling them afterwards that was tricky. I had to make them thick enough to be durable, but thin enough that they would light up the way I intended.

I started by taking Styrofoam balls and cutting the bases flat, so that the pumpkins would sit upright and still. Then I used my thumb to make an impression on the top that would serve as a niche for the stems to sit later. I wrapped the balls tightly in plastic wrap and put a small piece of tape on the bottom. I tinted some fondant with a touch of copper-colored gel food coloring to get a really light yellow orange color. I also kneaded in some Gum Tex powder, which makes the fondant a bit stronger—more like a gum paste. You can find Gum Tex at most cake supply stores that sell Wilton brand products. I rolled this fondant out to just a little over ¼" thick.

141

Working on one pumpkin at a time, I dusted the ball with cornstarch first. (This will make for easy removal later.) Then I covered the ball with the fondant and trimmed around the bottom. I picked the ball up and tucked in the fondant underneath; this helped give the pumpkin an open but more durable bottom. Next, I used a fondant tool to make the depressions for the lines of the pumpkin. You want to go deep enough to give it dimension; but at the same time, don't go too thin. Once I had the lines in, it was time to carve my pumpkins! I used an X-acto knife and carved in the faces. For the stems, I just used scraps and rolled them into little logs, then twisted them slightly for that realistic stem look.

Then I let them dry overnight on the Styrofoam balls in front of a fan. The next day, I brushed on some deeper orange-powdered food coloring. (I think I used "sunflower.") I also used a cocoa color to deepen the lines and then some moss green and cocoa to color the stems.

The next day, after they had dried enough to handle, I carefully cut them in half using the X-acto knife with as much of a clean cut as possible. Very gently, pull the halves apart and pull it off of the Styrofoam ball and the plastic. Once off of the form, it's time to put them back together. I just use an artist flat brush, dampen it with water, and go along each edge. Wait just a few seconds for the fondant to soften, then put the pieces back together. You can wait for a few minutes and then use a dampened brush again to smooth out any crumbs if necessary. I sat them back in front of the fan so that the insides could dry and harden.

For the stems, I actually waited until it was time to assemble the cake. I just barely moistened the bottom of the stem and then the top of the pumpkin and sat the stem gently on top without pressing

down. They were a great addition to the cake display and I just love the little guy's expression . . . I might just keep him because I feel so sorry for him.

Step 7: Making the Hard Candy and Pulled Sugar

This was a key element in my cake design. I have seen tons of fondant cauldron cakes, but all of them had buttercream icing for the "bubbling goo" and maybe some fondant body parts thrown in. I really wanted my goo to look more like a transparent liquid, and I knew without a doubt that it had to "glow." Well, if I could do that, then surely I could make fiery ambers as well, right? This was my first time working with cooked sugar of this type, my goal here was for the solid top, the little spurts, and the splashes of green pulled sugar were just for practice and, actually, came out surprisingly well for my first attempt.

Preparing the Molds

Finding a candy recipe was easy (there are tons on the net), but I had to figure out how to mold or shape it. For the green goo, I used a flat glass lid from one of my glass Pyrex bowls. Then I cut out pieces of a cardboard egg carton, trimmed them all lower than the lid, and then taped them on the bottoms so they wouldn't move around. Next, I used heavy duty aluminum foil to cover the whole thing and made depressions in the foil. I didn't want this too thick, so I kept the depressions shallow. I think it ended up being maybe ¼" to ½" thick. Be careful though—too thin and it will

break during assembly; too thick and it will be too heavy. (My piece was pretty heavy as it was.) After you're satisfied with the mold, spray lightly with a non-stick cooking spray.

- Hard candy (think lollipops)
- 1 cup white granulated sugar
- ½ cup light corn syrup
- ¼ cup water
- ¾ teaspoon extract flavoring (I used pineapple flavoring)
- Food coloring
- You'll also need a candy thermometer.

Combine the sugar, corn syrup, and water in a medium saucepan over medium heat and stir until sugar is dissolved. Place your thermometer into the pan, keeping it from resting on the bottom. Heat to a boil, without stirring, until candy reaches 295° to 300°F (hard crack stage). Remove from heat and quickly stir in your extract and food coloring. Immediately pour into molds. Let set at room temperature until candy hardens (it only takes a few hours). Store in a cool, dry place (not the refrigerator) covered with plastic wrap until ready to use.

For the Green Goo

I used just a few drops of neon green food coloring. After I poured it into my mold, I poured just a portion of it onto a Silpat mat. I let it cool until it was still soft but I could handle it. With gloves on, I pulled it just to get some sheen. Now, I really didn't know what I was doing here, I was just following how I've seen pulled sugar done. (This is a technique that is used to make sugar ribbons.) Then I pulled little pieces off and into long strands. For the spirals, I lightly sprayed a honing steel and, as I pulled a piece off, I quickly wrapped it around the honing steel. It set up rather quickly and then I was ready to slide it off. I made some other quirky shapes just so I would have pieces to stand up in

the cauldron goo, so I really didn't have to be so precise.

I did the green pieces way ahead of time (about one week prior to assembly), since this was my first time trying out these sugar techniques. If I use this technique again, I'll wait until it's closer to the time of assembly. My kitchen is really super humid and some of the delicate pieces either broke or melted, which, actually, I had expected anyway. This type of sugar art will take some practice but I will definitely revisit the idea at a later date. I waited until the entire cake display was assembled before attaching the spiral shapes to the top of the green goo. This was pretty easy because at this point, they were pretty sticky. It was just a matter of balancing them on there.

For the Coals

I used the top plastic part of the egg carton; but this time, I crumpled up a large piece of parchment paper, laid it over the tray, and made some more depressions. Be sure to let the paper rise above the plastic tray, else the sugar may be too hot for it and melt it (plus I didn't want my coals too big). Spray the parchment paper with nonstick cooking spray. I used the same recipe as above, except this time, I tried to throw in some powdered Kool-Aid mix to make an "orange pineapple" flavor (this was a tip I found on one of the sites). However, I would *not* recommend this—the candy was really bitter and I only used less than a teaspoon. The green one tasted much, much better and more like pineapple lollipops. Leave the coals in the paper mold until you are ready to use them because they will be sticky and they will melt and fuse together once they are touching.

Again, although I completed this step first, I decided to add it in here, where I would actually do it the next time.

144

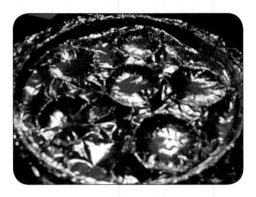

Step 8: Making the Cauldron Cake

While I've grouped certain steps together so that you can see how each component was done, I wanted to point out that I actually baked and prepared the cakes for both the tree and the cauldron a day before cake assembly. I just wrapped them well with plastic wrap and stored in the fridge until it was go time.

For the cauldron cake, it took three boxed cake mixes. I used two of the cake mixes to bake 2 9" round layers. Then, I used another box for the layer for the bottom of the cauldron in a glass Pyrex bowl (about 8" in diameter at the top and maybe 4" on the bottom). I only filled the bowl up about two-thirds of way and had left over batter (just bake this in a small layer pan or bake some cupcakes). I had also made my cardboard cake rounds (with the holes) the day ahead. I needed a smaller 4" one for the bottom and a 7" one for the top. I also drilled ¾" holes into the centers and then used white electrical tape (cake board tape) around the edges.

I trimmed all of the cakes to level them. In the photo, you can see I'm using a (Wilton) cake leveler, but you can also do this with a long serrated knife. I measured the height of each cake layer to give me an idea of how tall the cauldron would be. This was a crucial step at this point, because I didn't

want the cauldron to be taller than the witch's hand. (I could trim the cakes, but I couldn't move the arm or hand.) Also, I had to calculate how much filling would be added; plus I had to consider how tall the top candy portion would be; plus I wanted to make sure my pipe would hit right at the top of the cake layers.

After leveling the cakes, I cut holes in the center of each layer (I used the wide end of a pastry decorating tip). I took the two 9" rounds and put buttercream filling between them and stacked them, lining up the holes. Then I sat the 7" white cake board on top in the center and used it as a guide to round the top edges. I used a long serrated knife to carve in the edges.

Next, I gently turned those upside down so that the white 7" board is now on the bottom. I put more buttercream on what is facing up. Then I placed the "bowl cake" on, lined up the holes, and placed the smaller 4" round on top of that. I trimmed what will be the bottom of the cauldron into shape. Once I had the shape done (the cauldron is upside down at this point), I turned the whole thing right side up. So I had the 4" board on the bottom, the bowl cake, then the two 9" round layers, then the 7" white board.

Now, I iced the cake using a crusting buttercream. I wanted to use a crusting buttercream in lieu of fondant for two reasons. One, fondant would be way too heavy, and two, I was shooting for more of an "iron skillet" look to the cauldron. Here's the recipe I used.

Crusting Buttercream Icing

- 1 stick of butter (not margarine)
- 1 cup shortening
- 2 pound bag of confectioner's sugar (powdered sugar)
- ½ teaspoon salt
- 1 tablespoon meringue powder
- 1 teaspoon vanilla extract (or other extract flavorings of your choice)
- ½ teaspoon almond extract
- 3–4 tablespoons warm water (depends on consistency desired)

(For chocolate icing: Replace ½–¾ cup of the powdered sugar with Hershey's Unsweetened Cocoa.)

Cream your butter and shortening in a stand mixer. Add in the salt and extracts and beat well. Pour in about half of the powdered sugar and the meringue powder. If making chocolate, now is the time to add that in. Beat on high, occasionally stopping and scraping down sides of bowl. Add in a few tablespoons of the warm water and then start adding in the rest of the powdered sugar, ½ cup at a time, until all is used. The icing will be really thick, so you may add in more water if needed until you get a nice spreading consistency.

I iced the entire cake and waited for it to dry and crust on the outside. Then I used a small piece of parchment paper to gently lay over it and smooth it with my hands (or you could use a paper towel).

Next, I picked up the whole cake and slid it down onto the cake pipe on the cake board. Once it was in place, I brought the lights up out of the pipe that I had tucked in there and used white tape to tape them to the white 7" cake board (the picture below of the lights and board were actually taken during the deconstruction phase). This is where it's helpful to have a second set of hands and eyes.

Now, once the lights were secured, I made a large roll of fondant to go around the circumference of the white board. This also served as a "spacer" for the green top, which went on next.

After the cauldron was completely assembled, I covered my cake stand with paper to protect it from over spray and used a cake round just to cover the top green candy while I airbrushed it black. (I use Kroma brand airbrush food colorings.) Next, I placed the "coals" around the bottom, sticking some directly to the acrylic container first and then adding in some at the bottom and sticking those directly to the cake board paper.

Two mistakes I made:

1. I didn't think that the three layers would be so heavy. Therefore, I didn't add any supports such as dowels or straws between the layers. (I know better, I just got in a hurry.) I should have, because they were heavy. Especially when I added the weight of the candy piece. So the cake only held its shape for one day before it started to sag down. Next time, I would use a cake board with *each* layer and sink straws in each layer for added support.

2. The bottom white cake round wasn't big enough. When the cake started to settle, it sagged over the bottom cake round. Also, the cake started to tilt a bit.

Other than that, the lighting system was fantastic and worked according to my plan. I was also happy with the crusted iron pot look.

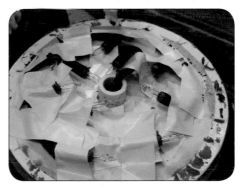

"roots" when transferring it over to the cake board. After leveling both layers of cake, I put them on the cake board and carved in some V shapes between each root (a real tree isn't perfectly round, right?). I used maple buttercream icing for the filling and then put a thin (¼") coat all over, except for the top.

Next, I added rolled pieces of black fondant to create the tree roots (the fondant was left over from the cauldron and witch). Next, I put another layer of icing on all over, including covering the roots and the top. Once the icing started to crust over, I began making my bark by carving in lines with a fondant tool. Then, I took a piece of parchment paper and laid it on the top of the trunk. I flattened the icing a bit with a fondant smoothing tool and then traced around just the inside edges of where the bark lines were.

I used that piece of paper as a pattern and cut out where I had traced. Then I rolled out some white fondant and cut out around the pattern. Next, I applied what was now to be the "cut portion" of the trunk and laid it into the buttercream icing, smoothing it and pushing it down into the icing. I want to point out that you could just cover the whole tree with fondant, carve the bark marks into the fondant, and then air brush. But I was testing the effects of a using a crusting buttercream. The top piece of fondant is necessary either way, because otherwise the fondant doo-dads would be too heavy and would have sunk into the trunk.

I left the paper on while I airbrushed the tree. I did a coat of a reddish brown first, followed by a coat of black. Next, I removed the paper pattern and airbrushed a little color of the brown and black. Before it dried, I used a wet flat brush to remove some of the color; this created the growth rings in the cut tree.

Step 9: Making the Tree Stump Cake

Well I must say, after what I went through with the cauldron, the tree stump was a piece of cake (sad pun intended). I also want to point out that I had done the ax, toad, spell book, and mortar and pestle at the time of making the pumpkins; this gave them plenty of time to dry.

For the tree cake, I baked 2 8" rounds. I cut my cake board so that it would have three points, in order to hold the fondant

When finished with the painting, I used a large heavy cake knife, slid it under the cake board, and transferred it to the cake stand. I had to, at the same time, use a smaller knife to hold one of the heavier limbs. To top it off, I added the doo-dads—the frog (and his cut leg), book, and mortar and pestle—and then just leaned the ax beside the tree.

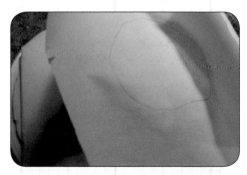

The greatest part was the official lighting of the cake. I tell ya, I felt like Clark Griswald on *National Lampoon's Christmas Vacation* . . . you know, the moment when he plugged in the Christmas lights for the house? Only, to my amazement, it totally worked the first time.

Step 10: Finishing up the Cake Display

So far, I have placed the cauldron and tree onto the cake board/stand. Next, it was time to add witchie-poo. Remember, I have her on a separate base, so it's just a matter of picking her up off of that base and threading her lighting wires through the pipe and flange that is already secured on the cake board. You'll definitely need an extra pair of hands for this step. I held the witch up while my daughter guided the wires through and pulled them underneath the board. Next, it was just a matter of reconnecting the previously cut wires back to the battery pack. Wrap them with electrical tape individually.

Lastly, I placed the pumpkins over their lights and sprinkled around some multi-bran flake cereal for the leaves. Originally, I really wanted to air brush them with fall colors, but again, I got in a hurry and just wanted to call it done.

Step 11: The Deconstruction Process

People always ask, "Is that really cake?" or "How can you cut it after all that work? No, wait . . . how *do* you cut it?" So, I thought it would be fun to actually, for the first time, document the deconstructing process. Firstly, to somewhat offer proof that, yes, it is indeed a real cake, not a "dummy cake." Secondly, that the deconstruction process isn't as bad or as messy as one might think.

Whenever I design a cake, I usually think about the carving and serving process as well. It's just a matter of following your building steps backwards. The tree stump is pretty self explanatory, just slice and carve as you would any other round cake.

For the cauldron, first I removed the candy top and fondant log ring and set them aside. I used a meat mallet to tap the large piece and break it up into smaller pieces. Next, I carefully removed the tape that was holding down the lights, then I pulled the light string out from underneath the cake stand. Next,

I removed the white cake board. After that I just basically positioned plates on both sides and cut the cake down the middle on each side of the pipe. One piece fell over and a little of the cake stuck to the bottom cake board, but really, no big deal. Then I just sliced each half into serving size portions.

As for witchie-poo, I wanted to save her and add her to my collection. I took her off and placed her back on the other stand safe and sound. I'll wait for a good month for her to dry out completely, then I'll spray her with a polyurethane lacquer to seal it and preserve it. You can store dried fondant pieces for who knows how long, as long as you keep them away from heat, moisture, and direct sun light.

In conclusion, I hope that someone has found this tutorial helpful. I also hope that, this being my very first official Instructable, I did a decent job writing it.

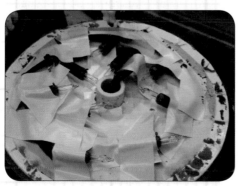

Section 6
Adventurous

Pirate Ship Cake

By Ericka Alicea

(erigeeka)

(http://www.instructables.com/
id/Pirate-Ship-Cake/)

I've made this cake twice now, and twice I've neglected to take pictures showing the process. This is just a demo of a larger scale cake I made last May for a birthday party. Since I didn't take pictures while making last year's cakes, and since I don't have a reason to make another large-scale pirate ship cake, I decided just to show the techniques using a store-bought pound cake.

Of course you don't have to use the same cake recipes as I did. You don't even have to make the cake from scratch; a store-bought cake mix brand will work just fine in making a totally awesome pirate ship cake.

The recipe I used for the first pirate ship cake was one I found from the *Barefoot Contessa Family Style* recipe book called Birthday Sheet Cake. I did alter her recipe slightly by adding orange zest instead of lemon zest, which is what she adds to her birthday sheet cake. The cake tasted just as good as it looked, believe it or not.

The second pirate ship cake I made is a vegan version with chocolate, raspberry, and cashew nut butter. The texture of this cake is super moist, which made it a little more difficult to build a pirate ship out of it. But it was the *best* tasting cake I've ever had.

The First Cake

For the Cake

- 18 tablespoons (2.25 sticks) unsalted butter, at room temperature
- 3 cups sugar
- 6 extra-large eggs, at room temperature
- 8 oz (about 1 cup) sour cream, at room temperature
- 1.5 teaspoons pure vanilla extract
- 1 lemon, zested
- 3 cups all-purpose flour
- ⅓ cup corn starch
- 1 teaspoon kosher salt
- 1 teaspoon baking soda

For the Frosting

- 24 oz semisweet chocolate chips
- 1.5 cups heavy cream
- 2 tablespoons light corn syrup
- ½ teaspoon pure vanilla extract
- 4 tablespoons (½ stick) unsalted butter, at room temperature

Preheat the oven to 350° F. Butter and flour a 12″ × 18″ × 1.5″ sheet pan. To make the cake, cream the butter and sugar on medium-high speed in the bowl of an electric mixer, fitted with a paddle attachment, until light and fluffy (about five minutes). On medium speed, add the eggs, two at a time, then the sour cream, vanilla, and lemon zest, scraping down the bowl as needed. Mix well. Sift together the flour, cornstarch, salt, and baking soda. With the mixer on low speed, slowly add the flour mixture to the butter mixture and stir just until smooth. Finish mixing by hand to be sure the batter is well mixed. Pour evenly into the pan, smooth the top with a spatula, and bake in the center of the oven for twenty-five to thirty minutes, or until a toothpick comes out clean. Cool in the pan to room temperature.

For the frosting, place the chocolate chips and heavy cream in a bowl set over a pot of simmering water, stirring occasionally, until the chips are completely melted. Off the heat, add the corn syrup and vanilla, and allow the chocolate mixture to cool to room temperature. In the bowl of an electric mixer fitted with the whisk attachment, whisk the chocolate mixture and softened butter on medium speed for a few minutes, until it's thickened. Spread the frosting evenly on the cake.

The Second Cake

The second pirate ship cake I made was using a tasty vegan recipe I found online from Moosewood Restaurant called Deep Chocolate Vegan Cake.

For the cake
- 1.5 cups unbleached white flour
- ⅓ cup unsweetened cocoa powder
- ½ teaspoon baking soda
- ½ teaspoon salt
- 1 cup sugar
- ½ cup vegetable oil (corn oil works as well)
- 1 cup cold water or chilled brewed coffee
- 2 teaspoons pure vanilla extract
- 2 tablespoons cider vinegar

Preheat oven to 375°. Generously oil an 8" square and dust with a little sifted cocoa, or line the bottom with parchment paper. In a medium bowl, sift together flour, cocoa, baking soda, salt, and sugar. In another bowl, combine the oil, water or coffee, and vanilla. Pour the liquid ingredients into the dry ingredients and mix until well blended and smooth. Add the vinegar and stir briefly. The baking soda will begin to react with the vinegar right away, leaving pale swirls in the batter. Quickly pour the batter into the baking pan.

Bake for twenty-five to thirty minutes. Cake is done when a toothpick inserted in the center comes out dry. Transfer to a plate when cool and glaze.

Chocolate Cashew Nut Butter Raspberry Glaze

In a double boiler or small, heavy saucepan over a medium flame, melt ⅓ cup raspberry jam with 1.5 cups carob chips or chocolate chips, mix thoroughly, and add 2 tablespoons of cashew nut butter (feel free to add more cashew nut butter if you desire a nuttier flavor) to the chocolate as it is melting. In another small saucepan, mix 4 tablespoons of jam with 1 tablespoon water and warm over a low flame until the spread liquefies. Brush the water-fruit mixture over the top of cooled cake. Spread the chocolate/cashew butter nut mixture on top of that. Allow the glaze to cool before cutting the cake. Serves eight.

Step 1: What You'll Need
- Toy pirates (I found mine at a local party store)
- Candles
- Malt balls (these are your cannons)
- Pepperidge Farm Pirouette Chocolate Crème Filled Rolled Wafer Cookies (any brand or flavor is fine
- Drinking straws
- Wood skewers
- Ice cream cone
- 12" × 18" × 1.5" sheet pan or an 8" square baking pan depending on what size cake you want

- Colored construction paper to make the sails
- Sword-shaped cocktail stir sticks (I found these also at my local party store)

You want to make sure you have a sturdy surface to work on. For the first pirate ship cake I used a cake board to place my cake on, which I coved in a cool pirate themed bandanna. You can purchase a cake board at Sur La Table or Williams and Sonoma. Basically it's a piece of cardboard, which you don't necessarily have to buy. For the second pirate ship cake I made, I just used a baking sheet that I covered in foil.

Step 2: Shaping the Cake— Part 1
Don't even try shaping the cake until it has had a significant amount of time to cool. Cut the cake long ways, completely down the middle.

Step 3: Shaping the Cake— Part 2

Now you have two halves of cake. Put the two halves back together and cut off the bottom portion as shown in the photos. This adds height to the pirate ship when making it out of the sheet cake.

Step 4: Frosting

Frost the insides of the large pieces of cake and place them on top of each other.

Step 5: Adding the Two Other Pieces

The remaining pieces of cake are secured at the edges using a wooden skewer.

Step 6: Slant the Top Edges and Then Frost the Rest of the Ship

The two pieces you just secured using the wooden skewers need to have a slight slant to them to add to the ship-like appearance. This demo cake doesn't have much of a slant because there wasn't much cake to work with. But when you make your pirate ship cake using a sheet cake that is much bigger, you will be able to create a noticeable slant. Use a sharp knife to get this effect. I forgot to include a picture of shaping the front of the ship. The end you choose to make the front portion of your ship should have its edges slightly shaved. You can now frost the rest of the cake.

Step 7: Building the Bottom Portion of the Crow's Nest

Place a regular drinking straw inside the pirouette cookie, leaving about three inches of the straw exposed. Now place the straw end into the middle of the ship, making sure it goes in a few inches. You want to make sure the bottom portion of the crow's nest is in securely so it doesn't bend.

Step 8: Building the Top Portion of the Crow's Nest

First, get your ice cream cone and gently cut the top portion off with a sharp knife. You may go through one or two cones if you're not gentle enough. Now make a small hole inside the bottom of the cone. Place the cone on top of the bottom portion of the crow's nest. Next, push another straw entirely through another cookie. This is so you can push out some of the chocolate filling that's inside of the cookie. You can now place the second cookie inside the crow's nest.

161

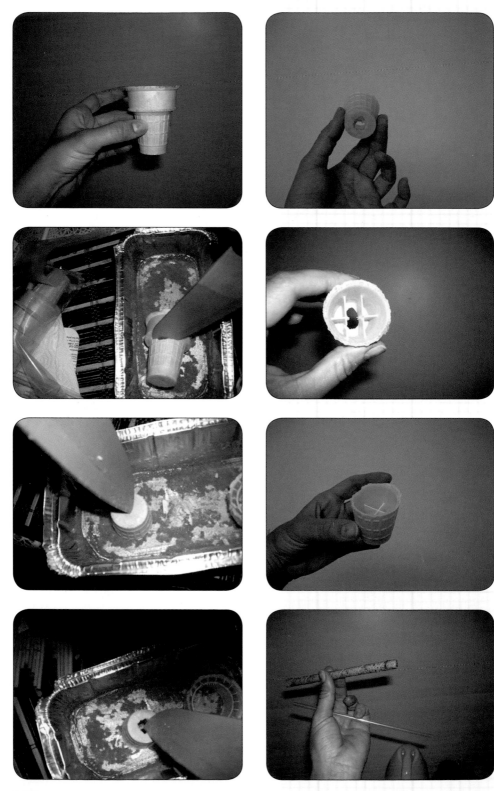

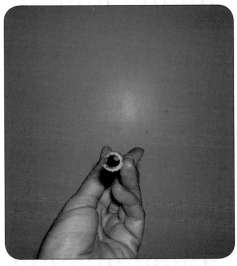

construction paper. I poked the wooden skewer at both ends of the sail and then pushed it into the cake. You will learn that you'll have to keep re-frosting due to smudges and also to use as a glue. I stuck a toy pirate inside the crow's nest and used the frosting as a glue. The frosting also helped me glue together my malt ball cannon clusters. Enjoy!

Step 9: Decorating Your Totally Awesome Pirate Ship Cake!

Decorate your cake using the toy pirates, malt balls, cocktail stir stick swords, and pirouette cookies. I gave my cake a wood grain appearance by using a fork. I made the sails out of regular

Erupting Volcano Birthday Cake

By Dave Spencer
(dave spencer)
(http://www.instructables.com/id/
erupting-volcano-birthday-cake/)

For my son's fifth birthday, I decided to go a little nuts. Four months and about $200 later, I believe I created something one of a kind. I wanted a volcano that would do several things:

- smoke
- erupt with lava
- vibrate
- and finally, make volcano noises.

Step 1: Lava

I was thinking of making my own piston-type lava delivery system, but then I realized I had a perfectly good one sitting around the house already. We have a chocolate fountain we bought for $75 a year ago. Everything for the cake was built around this. The actual lava was made by blending a $10 bulk bag of frozen strawberries with some icing, sugar, and cornstarch. This was reduced on the stove to thicken. The flow rate was tested and the sauce

was frozen. This was a mistake because I think freezing the sauce changed its consistency slightly and it did not flow as well as I would have liked on the big day.

Step 2: Making the Pan

The pan was made from an old stainless counter top. I cut and welded the pan with an angle grinder and a tig welder. The hole was cut with a drill and a hole saw. I ended up building a tower on top to extend the volcano higher and to reduce the volume of cake required.

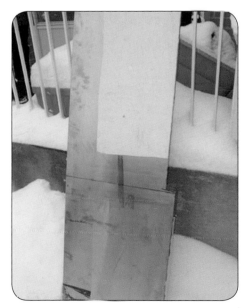

Step 4: Making It Vibrate

I took a motor for a power wheels jeep, welded a clamp, and offset the counterweight. It had to be clamped very securely to the box to transfer all of the vibrations. The motor was powered by a 12v power supply. The power supply for this and all other electric devices were switched on by a remote control that is used for Christmas tree lights. This worked awesome and actually shook the whole table the cake was sitting on.

Step 3: The Box

The box to hold everything was made from ⅝" thick MDF. I used a flapper disk on my grinder to round the edges and it worked really well. I painted the box with a textured spray paint that looks like rock. I welded the handles up and mounted them a little off center to compensate for the weight of the fountain inside.

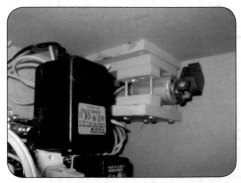

Step 5: Making Smoke

Smoke may be a bit misleading, but this was actually the most spectacular part of the show. It was made from a teaspoon of coco powder in two "shooters" powered by balloons. Each balloon sat in a holder hidden inside the box. A pin held the balloon in place. A slow turning motor pulled a string attached to the pin. (The motor turned too slow at first, so I added the arms to increase the radius.) Once pulled, the air rushes through tubing to the pan. Inside the tower of the pan is a loop in the tube. This holds the coco powder close to the end and allows me to separate the tubes between the pan and the box without the coco spilling out the bottom. When this went off, we somehow got four bursts out of two shooters. I still don't know how it happened, but I guess it is better to get more than you expected than less.

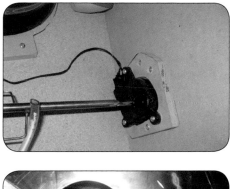

Step 6: Creating the Sounds

To sound like a volcano, I mixed sounds I found on the net. I combined the sounds of a fireworks show, bubbling soup, and rolling thunder. To play the sounds, I used an iPod Nano hooked up to an old set of computer speakers. The Nano played a continuous loop of the sound effects, and, when the power was turned on via the remote, the speakers turned on and the sounds could be heard clearly even in a crowded bowling alley. The picture here shows how everything fit into the box.

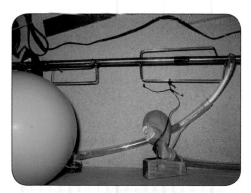

Step 7: The Cake!

This part took me about eight hours, seven cake mixes, and eleven cans of icing. I have made my own cakes and icings from scratch before, but this time I just wanted to get it done quickly (if you call eight hours quick). You can see two tubes for the coco powder shooters hanging below. They are visible sticking out the top of the volcano if you look closely. I also dusted the top of the volcano with icing sugar to make it look kind of snowy (not shown in this picture). I placed enough plastic dinosaurs (bought in packs of six from the dollar store) around the volcano so that every child at the party would get one with their slice. I made sure to place a few of the dinosaurs in the path the lava would take. What a project!

Well, since pirates are all the rage right now and my son loves them, we did a pirate theme for his birthday this year. As I was looking on how to make a pirate ship cake, I noticed there weren't too many detailed instructions on how to do this, just pictures of the finished cake. So I put this together to help inspire people to get creative with their cakes! Have fun and I hope you enjoy this Instructable as much as I did doing it!

Step 1: Making the Cake

First of all, you always want to make sure you have enough cake to make your idea come to life. For this cake I baked a 9" × 13" cake, an 8" × 8" square cake, and an 8" oval cake. The right cake plate is a big part of your cake also, because It makes for the perfect presentation and that "ooh, ahh" factor. So for this cake, I used a silver platter I had that is actually for a turkey or ham—it was perfect! Then I proceeded to place the

pieces, cut where necessary, and form the shape of the cake. On this cake, I used a chocolate buttercream frosting and made chocolate mousse for the filling between layers.

Step 2: Forming of the Cake

Basically, I started visualizing how I wanted the cake to look and went from there. The birthday boy was very happy about his cake!

Step 3: Frosting Time

Now, you just frost and add some jewels and finishing touches. For the jewels, I used M&Ms. For the rails of the ship, I used cereal straws since they are cheaper then Pirouettes.

Step 4: Working on Finishing Touches

Well, the finishing touches are usually the best part of the cake. That's when the creative juices start flowing. I used the pirates and cannon from an Imaginext pirate ship and used an Oreo for the ship's wheel. The ship's sails were fun to make. I used black construction paper and cut out the shape I wanted, with a slight circular shape cut into the sides. Then, I crumpled the paper and cut holes. I found an image of a skull and crossbones online, printed it, and glued it on. Quick note: Make sure to glue it on before you crumple your paper. Next, I added them to the skewer. For the front, I put one skewer at an angle and ran fishing line to the next one to put that sail at an angle.

Step 5: Setting the Table

Well, here is the table when all was said and done. We had the token skull and a fabulous pirate chest that we filled with the loot for the kids. For a unique touch, we took a silver candle holder, put a foam ball on top with floral tape, covered it with moss, and stuck skewers of dino nuggets in it. I had a jeweled tray I filled with fruit to add to the festivities. I sprinkled gold (plastic) coins and skulls and bones over the table.

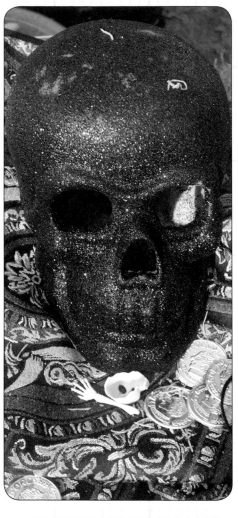

Section 7

Just Plain Adorable

Rainbow Swirl Cake

By Katrina Bahl
(inkatrinaskitchen)
(http://www.instructables.com/
id/Rainbow-Swirl-Cake/)

This cake is easy to make and fun to eat—perfect for birthdays or any colorful celebration. Frosted simply with white buttercream and decorated with rainbow nonpareils, your guests will have no idea what is in store for them when they cut into this cake.

Ingredients

• Yellow or white cake batter, divided
• Gel food dye (I use Americolor)
• Buttercream frosting

Step 1

Prepare your cake batter as you normally would and divide it into however many sections that you would like. I used a boxed yellow cake mix for this particular cake.

Step 2

Use food dye to color your cake batter. If you use gel or paste, then you will only need one drop per section for a brilliant, deep color. I used six colors for this cake. The possibilities are endless! Drop your batter into the pan(s) one color at a time and bake as you normally would. You can give the batter a little swirl with the tip of a knife if desired, but it isn't necessary.

Step 3

After baking and cooling, remove your cake(s) and frost simply with a white buttercream. Decorate with mini and jumbo rainbow nonpareils.

Creating rainbow food is fun because it brings out the kid in everyone. Boys and girls alike would love cutting into this surprise cake. As I said, if you use gel food coloring, you just need a tiny drop to achieve a deep, brilliant color.

Spools of Thread Cake Pops

By Xiaolu Hou

(6bittersweets)

(http://www.instructables.com/
id/Spools-of-Thread-Cake-Pops/)

I made these chocolate cookies and cream (Oreo) cake pops to look like spools of thread for a vintage-sewing-themed kids' birthday party.

Step 1

This Instructable makes about 20 to 23 lollipops. I strongly recommend making your own cake and frosting from scratch, as it allows you to control the sweetness of the pops much more. You may even want to reduce the amount of sugar from your usual cake since the candy coating will be quite sweet. Please don't be intimidated by my recipe. Its long length is mostly due to the inclusion of detailed notes/tips to make the process go as smoothly as possible. Store-bought fondant can be substituted for the marshmallow fondant, but marshmallow fondant tastes much, *much* better (pretty much like what you'd imagine from its ingredients).

Ingredients

- Marshmallow fondant (recipe at the end in the last step)
- Powdered sugar, for rolling fondant
- Round cookie cutter (1.5" wide)
- 8" or 9" cake layer (in a flavor of your choosing)
- ¼ to ¾ cups frosting (in a flavor of your choosing)
- 1 pound 2 oz candy melts or white chocolate chips/bark
- 1.5 tablespoons trans-fat-free shortening (such as Spectrum or Earth Balance)
- Canola or vegetable oil, as needed, to thin candy coating
- About twenty-one to twenty-four paper lollipop sticks (I use 4" sticks)
- Oil-based candy coloring or powder food coloring, optional

Step 2

While your cakes are baking, generously dust a large flat surface with powdered sugar. Roll out marshmallow fondant to a thickness of about ⅒". Dust top of fondant and rolling pin lightly with powdered sugar as needed to prevent sticking. Dip cookie cutter in powdered sugar and cut out as many 1.5" wide fondant circles as possible. Rub circles lightly with powdered sugar to prevent sticking. Repeat with additional fondant until you have twice as many fondant circles as cake pops. Make holes in the middle of half the fondant circles using a lollipop stick. First press the stick firmly into the middle of a fondant circle, then slide the circle up the stick while rotating the stick to slightly enlarge the circle.

Leave all fondant circles out to air dry while preparing the cake pops.

Step 3

Line two large baking pans with nonstick silicone mats or parchment paper. Crumble the cooled cake into a large bowl, removing any overcooked/crusty pieces. Add in ¼ cup of frosting and mix into the cake crumbs thoroughly, using clean fingers. Test the mixture by attempting to press and roll it into a 1.5" diameter ball. If the mixture crumbles instead of holding together as a ball, add more frosting—1 tablespoon at a time—mixing thoroughly and testing for consistency after each addition until mixture is moist enough to hold its shape.

Step 4

Now roll/press the cake the cookie mixture into balls 1.5" wide. Repeat until the cake mixture has been used up (you should have between 20 and 23 balls), and set the balls at least 1" apart from each other on a lined pan. Place cake balls in the freezer for 15 to 20 minutes.

Step 5

Remove cake balls from freezer and use both hands to press and shape into cylinders roughly 1.5" tall and 1" wide. I do this by first rolling the ball between both palms of my hands to elongate it slightly. Then I place the cake ball in the middle of my left palm and bring my fingers together around it as if making a fist while, *at the same time*, flattening the ends of the cake cylinder by pressing the open ends using the fingers of my right hand. Finally, I pinch the edges of both ends to create a more defined cylinder shape. Return the pan of cake cylinders to the freezer for 10 minutes.

Step 6

Place candy melts and 1.5 tablespoons of shortening into a heatproof bowl and microwave for one minute on medium heat. Stir well, then continue microwaving at 30-second intervals on medium heat, stirring between each, until the mixture is mostly melted and smooth. Continue stirring (but without beating—to avoid air bubbles in your coating) until the mixture becomes completely smooth. Dip the tip of each lollipop stick into a little melted coating and insert halfway (not more!) into the middle of each cake cylinder. Place in the fridge (not the freezer) for ten to fifteen minutes to firm up so the cake won't fall off the stick when coated.

Step 7

Meanwhile, color your coating with oil-based or powdered food coloring (not liquid or gel) in whatever shade you want your "thread" to be. (You can see from the photos that I didn't color the coating until after the base coat, which was okay but resulted in me piping on extra "thread" to cover up the white base. If you color your base coat, you won't have to worry about that!) Now pour your melted coating into a clean and dry cup that's about 2.5" wide until the cup is very close to full.

Step 8

Remove cake pops from the fridge and let sit for 10 minutes at room temperature (dipping the pops while cold will result in cracking of the coating because the cake will expand as it warms up). Dip an entire pop straight down into the melted candy coating until it is completely covered, and immediately remove it in one straight upward motion. (If you stir it around, the cake will fall off and it'll be very hard to salvage!) Once you lift the cake pop out of the coating, immediately turn the pop so that its stick is almost vertical with the cake pop pointing upwards. Make sure the coating meets at the base of the lollipop stick. This helps secure the cake ball to the stick when the coating sets.

Step 9

There will be extra coating still on the cake pop that you can remove. Hold the pop in one hand and use the other hand to gently tap the first wrist. Rotate the pop to allow the excess coating to drip evenly back into the cup of coating, but never let the stick tilt too far down or the cake may fall off. If too much coating collects at the base of the lollipop stick, you can wipe the excess off with a finger while rotating the stick. And if the coating seems too thick, stir in vegetable oil 1 teaspoon at a time until you get the desired consistency. When most of the extra coating has fallen off and no longer drips, turn the cake pop over again, so that the cake is down and the stick is up, and place it onto the second lined pan, making sure to set it down so that the stick points as straight up as possible. Repeat with the remaining cake pops. If the coating in the cup gets so low that you cannot easily submerge the whole cake pop, add more coating to the cup. If the coating in the cup hardens, transfer it back to the heatproof bowl and microwave for 20 seconds at a time on medium power, stirring well in between, *only* until the coating is fluid enough to dip again. Once all of the cake pops have been dipped in coating, let them set (harden) completely at room temperature or in the freezer (about eight minutes).

Step 10

Spoon about ⅔ cup of the leftover melted candy coating into a small zipper sandwich bag. Push as much air out of the bag as possible and seal the top. Cut a very small opening (about 1/10" wide) in one corner of the bag. Hold one cake pop near the base of its stick and over top of the empty baking pan (the one that used to hold the uncoated cake balls earlier). Make sure to hold the cake pop sideways so that all parts are the same distance from the pan under it. Pick up the bag with candy coating using your other hand. Squeeze the bag steadily while moving the opening back and forth quickly across the cake pop to create lines of "thread." Pipe the coating very wide so that it goes beyond the sides of the cake pop. This will result in a lot of the coating falling onto the pan underneath but will create more realistic looking "thread." Set the pop back down where it came from with the stick pointing up. Repeat with remaining cake pops. If the coating in the bag hardens, place bag on a microwave-safe plate and heat for twenty seconds on medium power. If the coating in the bag runs out, spoon more leftover coating into the bag or reheat/reuse coating that's dripped onto the pan if necessary. Let all cake pops set (harden) completely at room temperature or in the freezer (about 8 minutes).

Step 11

Again using the sandwich bag with melted coating, pipe a small dollop of coating on the bottom of a fondant circle (one without a hole).

Step 12

Spread the coating slightly with a small spoon, then immediately center a cake pop above the circle and press down lightly. Repeat with the remaining cake pops.

179

Step 13

Now, pipe a ring of candy coating around the outer edge at the top of each cake pop and let set (harden) completely at room temperature or in the freezer (about five minutes). The purpose of this is to create a more level top surface for the remaining fondant circles to stick to.

Step 14

Next, pipe a small amount of coating on the bottom of a fondant circle (with hole).

Step 15

Carefully turn the circle upside down while holding it by the edges, then slide the circle down the cake pop stick. Gently press down on the fondant with your fingers to make sure it sticks to the cake pop. Finally, lift the edges of the upper fondant circle slightly so that it is as flat as possible to resemble a spool. Repeat with remaining cake pops. Let cake pops set completely, then enjoy!

Step 16

Marshmallow Fondant
Adapted from Allrecipes.com
Makes about 1 pound 2 oz

You will only need about a third to a half of this recipe for the spools of thread cake pops, but this fondant keeps well in an airtight container and can be used just as other fondant is used.

- 2 tablespoons trans-fat-free shortening
- 8 oz miniature marshmallows
- 2 tablespoons water
- ½ tsp pure vanilla extract
- 1 pound powdered sugar, divided

Place the shortening in a shallow bowl that's easy to reach your hand into; then set aside.

Place the marshmallows in a large microwave-safe bowl, and microwave on high power for thirty seconds to one minute to start melting the marshmallows. Carefully stir the water and vanilla extract into the hot marshmallows until the mixture is smooth. If not yet smooth, continue microwaving at 20-second intervals and stirring thoroughly in between until smooth. Slowly beat in the powdered sugar, a cup at a time, until you have a sticky dough. Reserve 2 cups of powdered sugar for kneading.

Rub your hands thoroughly with shortening, and begin kneading the sticky dough. As you knead, the dough will become workable and pliable. Turn the dough out onto a working surface well-dusted with powdered sugar and continue kneading until the fondant is smooth and no longer sticky to the touch, which should take about five to ten minutes.

Form the fondant into a ball, rub a light film of shortening over the outside, wrap it tightly in plastic wrap, and refrigerate it overnight. To use, allow the fondant to come to room temperature, and roll it out on a flat surface dusted with powdered sugar. To make fondant more pliable, rub your fingers with more shortening and knead into the fondant.

Pastel Rainbow Ruffle Cake

By Linda Vandermeer

(BubbleandSweet)

(http://www.instructables.com/
id/Pastel-Rainbow-Ruffle-Cake/)

This oh-so-pretty pastel rainbow ruffle cake takes a little bit of time to put together, but the wow factor once it's finished is so worth it. You can use packet mix cake and frosting or whip up your own favorite recipes and then just follow the easy steps to make rows of ruffle-y sweetness. The ingredients and equipment for this cake can be found at large craft and hobby stores, cake specialty stores, and even on eBay.

Ingredients and Equipment
- 3 boxes of white cake mix (or make your own using your favorite recipe)
- Shop-bought white buttercream or frosting (or make your own using your favorite recipe)
- Rolled fondant or Pettince, 44 oz*
- Pink, violet, blue, green, and yellow gel food color (I used Wilton)
- Large rolling pin

- Corn flour (corn starch)
- Small rolling pin
- Large knife for trimming the cake
- Small sharp knife
- 2 cake smoothers
- Frilling tool—if you do not have a frilling tool, a toothpick can be used for a similar result.
- Nonstick flower molding mat
- Small brush and water

The night before decorating the cake, color the fondant with the gel colors as follows: 8 oz pink, 4 oz violet, 4 oz light blue, 4 oz light green, and 4 oz light yellow. The remaining 20 oz should remain plain white.

To color fondant, knead until soft and then add the gel food color a drop at a time, kneading well until the desired color is achieved. Store in an airtight container until ready to use.

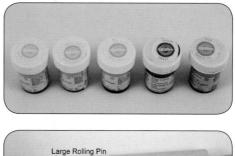

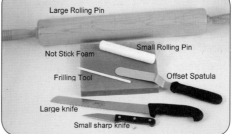

Step 1: Mix the Food Coloring and Bake the Cakes

Grease and flour your baking tins; if you like you can line them as well. You will need to bake five separate cakes for

---

*Fondant dries out really quickly—keep it in an airtight container or Zip-loc bag in between use and work really quickly.

182

the different layers, but if you only have one or two 8" baking tins, that is okay. Just grease and flour the tins you have and, once you have baked a cake and the tin has cooled down, you can wipe them out and reuse for the next colors.

Make up the cake batter and divide the mixture evenly between five bowls. Add ¼ teaspoon of the pink gel food color to the first bowl and mix until it is combined and there are no streaks. If you need to, add more color until you have achieved a pretty pastel color. Any of the mix you are not baking straight away (because you don't have enough pans or room in your oven), pop into the fridge.*

Repeat this process for the four remaining bowls of cake batter, adding violet to one, light green to another, yellow to another, and light blue to the final batch.

Pour each separate mixture into a separate baking tin and then bake in an oven following the directions on the packet mix box. Check 10 minutes prior to the recommended baking time by inserting a toothpick or skewer into the cake to see if it is cooked through. If it is not cooked through, continue to bake for 5–10 minutes until no crumbs stick to the toothpick or skewer.

Once the cakes are cooked, remove them from the oven. Leave in the pan for five minutes and then turn out onto a wire rack to cool.

Step 2: Stack the Cakes and Cover in Buttercream

Trim the top and bottom off each layer to make the cake flat and remove the thin brownish crust. Take the cake board and, starting with the yellow cake layer for the base, pop a little of the butter cream in the center to secure the cake. Then, add a layer of the white frosting or buttercream, add the green cake layer, and pop the cake into the fridge for 10 to 15 minutes to chill. Start to stack each of the rainbow layers of cake, adding a layer of frosting or buttercream in between each layer.

Once the final pink cake layer is in place and chilled, spread a thin layer of buttercream around the edges and made the cake as smooth as possible. Well, as smooth as possible without going overboard—remember, there will be lots of ruffles covering this cake. Chill the cake again until the buttercream is firm. At this stage, take a piece of paper and mark on it where each different layer of cake ends/starts to use as a guide for the ruffles.

*Popping the unbaked cake batter mixture in the fridge will slow down any type of "baking" reaction due to mixing the ingredients together.

Step 3: Cover the Cake with Fondant

Cover the cake with the fondant under layer for the ruffles to stick on. Measure around the cake with a piece of string to work out how long your fondant will need to be, and then measure the height. You will need to roll out a piece of fondant that you can cut into a rectangle the size that you have measured. Roll out the white fondant on a workbench dusted with a little corn flour (corn starch). Turn and lift the fondant often to make sure it does not stick and try and roll it out in a rectangular (ish) shape.

Once the fondant is big enough, trim along the top to get a straight line. Take the cake out of the fridge and lay it sideways onto the fondant so that you can wrap the fondant around the cake. Where the fondant joins at the back, you can wrap one layer over the other and then, using a sharp knife, cut down in a straight line. Lift up the fondant and remove any excess underneath and smooth the cut line together with your finger. Don't get too uptight about

making the finish really smooth, it's all going to be covered with ruffles. Pop the cake upright and use the sharp knife to trim off the fondant from around the bottom of the cake, and use fondant smoothers to make sure that the cake is smooth.

Take the pink fondant and roll it out on a corn flour (corn starch) dusted work bench until very thin and, using the cake tin that you used to bake the cakes in, press down to cut out around the approximate size of the cake. Place it on top of the cake and use the fondant smoothers to make the top as smooth as you can.

Take the piece of paper where you marked where the cake layers started and ended and, using a knife, make a little indent so you will know where each color ends/starts to use as a guide for your ruffles.

Step 4: How to Make the Ruffles

Starting with the pink fondant, dust the workbench with corn flour (corn starch), take a piece of fondant about 1.5 teaspoons, and shape it into a rectangle. Using the small rolling pin, roll it out into a long strip. As you roll, you may need to press the sides in carefully with the sides/heels of your hands to stop it from getting too wide. (Or if you find that is not working, you can always use a sharp knife to trim it back to size.) Keep rolling until the strip is quite thin. I like to pick the strip up after each roll to ensure it is not sticking to the bench and, when necessary, dust underneath again.

When you have rolled out the fondant as thin as you can on the workbench, pick up the strip of fondant and place it onto a nonstick foam (the type you use for making fondant flowers). Using the middle section of the frilling tool, roll back and forth (like using a rolling pin) to make the strip even thinner. You will probably get it to double in length. Then, use the pointed edge of the frilling tool a little more, rolling it back and forth along one edge of the strip, to make it a little ruffle-y.

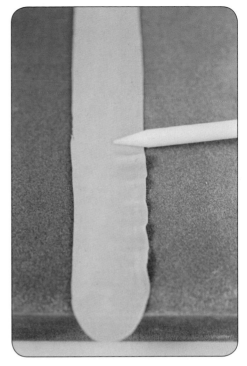

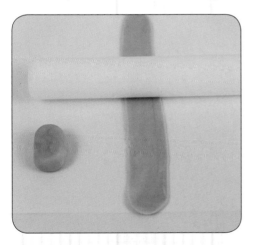

Step 5: Applying the Ruffles to the Cake

Attach the ruffles, starting at the top of the cake and working down. Brush on a very small amount of water to the cake along the top and press the fondant strip onto the cake. You can gather the strip to make it appear more ruffle-y (see picture). When you have finished attaching one strip, make another and attach it to the cake starting where the last strip finished. Go back and press the lumpy bottoms of the ruffles down as you finish attaching each strip.

Continue making pink strips of fondant and attaching them to the cake, working your way down the cake until you reach the indent, indicating that you should start with the next color and follow the instructions violet ruffles this time. Follow this process for all the remaining colors until the cake is completely covered with ruffles.

As you work your way down, some of the ruffles may fall down and look floppy.

You can brush a tiny amount of water around the middle section of the fallen ruffle and press it up so it is upright, but this look is not about perfection so some floppy areas will work just fine. At the very bottom of the cake, roll out a strip of yellow around one-third of the width of the regular strips and, without ruffling it, adhere it around the bottom to cover any of the uneven ruffle bottoms and make a clean finish.

Cake can be made the day before serving and stored at room temperature. Do not store in a fridge or put in an airtight container (butte creams that require refrigeration will not be suitable for this cake).

Now you can slice into it and enjoy.

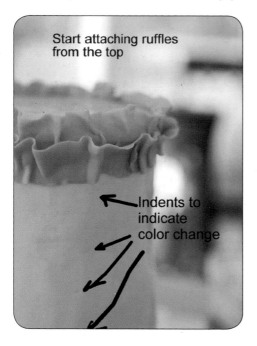

Start attaching ruffles from the top

Indents to indicate color change

CONVERSION TABLES

One person's inch is another person's centimeter. Instructables projects come from all over the world, so here's a handy reference guide that will help keep your project on track.

Measurement									
	1 Millimeter	1 Centimeter	1 Meter	1 Inch	1 Foot	1 Yard	1 Mile	1 Kilometer
Millimeter	1	10	1,000	25.4	304.8	—	—	—
Centimeter	0.1	1	100	2.54	30.48	91.44	—	—
Meter	0.001	0.01	1	0.025	0.305	0.91	—	1,000
Inch	0.04	0.39	39.37	1	12	36	—	—
Foot	0.003	0.03	3.28	0.083	1	3	—	—
Yard	—	0.0109	1.09	0.28	033	1	—	—
Mile	—	—	—	—	—	—	1	0.62
Kilometer	—	—	1,000	—	—	—	1.609	1

Volume									
	1 Mil-liliter	1 Liter	1 Cubic Meter	1 Tea-spoon	1 Tablespoon	1 Fluid Ounce	1 Cup	1 Pint	1 Quart	1 Gal-lon
Milliliter	1	1,000	—	4.9	14.8	29.6	—	—	—	—
Liter	0.001	1	1,000	0.005	0.015	0.03	0.24	0.47	0.95	3.79
Cubic Meter	—	0.001	1	—	—	—	—	—	—	0.004
Teaspoon	0.2	202.9	—	1	3	6	48	—	—	—
Tablespoon	0.068	67.6	—	0.33	1	2	16	32	—	—
Fluid Ounce	0.034	33.8	—	0.167	0.5	1	8	16	32	—
Cup	0.004	4.23	—	0.02	0.0625	0.125	1	2	4	16
Pint	0.002	2.11	—	0.01	0.03	0.06	05	1	2	8
Quart	0.001	1.06	—	0.005	0.016	0.03	0.25	.05	1	4
Gallon	—	0.26	264.17	0.001	0.004	0.008	0.0625	0.125	0.25	1

conversion tables

Mass and Weight						
	1 Gram	1 Kilogram	1 Metric Ton	1 Ounce	1 Pound	1 Short Ton
Gram	1	1,000	—	28.35	—	—
Kilogram	0.001	1	1,000	0.028	0.454	—
Metric Ton	—	0.001	1	—	—	0.907
Ounce	0.035	35.27	—	1	16	—
Pound	0.002	2.2	—	0.0625	1	2,000
Short Ton	—	0.001	1.1	—	—	1

Speed		
	1 Mile per hour	1 Kilometer per hour
Miles per hour	1	0.62
Kilometers per hour	1.61	1

Temperature		
	Fahrenheit (°F)	Celsius (°C)
Fahrenheit	—	(°C x 1.8) + 32
Celsius	(°F − 32) / 1.8	—

also available

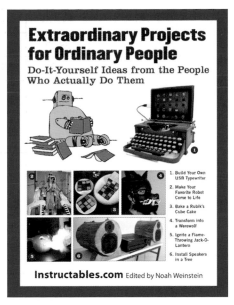

Extraordinary Projects for Ordinary People
Do-It-Yourself Ideas from the People Who
Actually Do Them
by Instructables.com, edited by Noah Weinstein

Collected in this volume is a best-of selection from
Instructables, reproduced for the first time outside of
the web format, retaining all of the charm and ingenuity
that make Instructables such a popular destination for
Internet users looking for new and fun projects designed by real people in an easy-to-digest way.

Hundreds of Instructables are included, ranging from
practical projects like making a butcher-block counter-
top or building solar panels to fun and unique ideas for
realistic werewolf costumes or transportable camping
hot tubs. The difficulty of the projects ranges from beginner on up, but all are guaranteed to raise a smile or
a "Why didn't I think of that?"

US $16.95 paperback ISBN: 978-1-62087-057-0

also available

How to Do Absolutely Everything
Homegrown Projects from Real Do-It-Yourself Experts
by Instructables.com, edited by Sarah James

Continuing the Instructables series with Skyhorse Publishing, a mammoth collection of projects has been selected and curated for this special best-of volume of Instructables. The guides in this book cover the entire spectrum of possibilities that the popular website has to offer, showcasing how online communities can foster and nurture creativity.

From outdoor agricultural projects to finding new uses for traditional household objects, the beauty of Instructables lies in their ingenuity and their ability to find new ways of looking at the same thing. *How to Do Absolutely Everything* has that in spades; the possibilities are limitless, thanks to not only the selection of projects available here, but also the new ideas you'll build on after reading this book. Full-color photographs illustrate each project in intricate detail, providing images of both the individual steps of the process and the end product.

US $16.95 paperback ISBN: 978-1-62087-066-2

also available

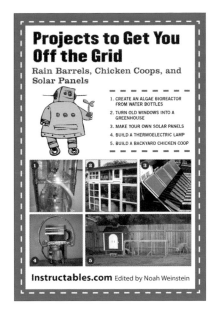

Projects to Get You Off the Grid
Rain Barrels, Chicken Coops, and Solar Panels
by Instructables.com, edited by Noah Weinstein

Instructables is back with this compact book focused on a series of projects designed to get you thinking creatively about thinking green. Twenty Instructables illustrate just how simple it can be to make your own backyard chicken coop or turn a wine barrel into a rainwater collector.

Illustrated with dozens of full-color photographs per project accompanying easy-to-follow instructions, this Instructables collection utilizes the best that the online community has to offer, turning a far-reaching group of people into a mammoth database churning out ideas to make life better, easier, and, in this case, greener, as this volume exemplifies.

US $14.95 paperback ISBN: 978-1-62087-164-5

also available

Backyard Rockets

Learn to Make and Launch Rockets, Missiles, Cannons, and Other Projectiles

by Instructables.com, edited by Mike Warren

Originating from Instructables, a popular project-based community made up of all sorts of characters with wacky hobbies and a desire to pass on their wisdom to others, *Backyard Rockets* is made up of projects from a medley of authors who have collected and shared a treasure trove of rocket-launching plans and the knowledge to make their projects soar!

Backyard Rockets gives step-by-step instructions, with pictures to guide the way, on how to launch your very own project into the sky. All of these authors have labored over their endeavors to pass their knowledge on and make it easier for others to attempt.

US $12.95 paperback ISBN: 978-1-62087-730-2

also available

Unusual Uses for Ordinary Things
250 Alternative Ways to Use Everyday Items
by Instructables.com, edited by Wade Wilgus

Most people use nail polish remover to remove nail polish. They use coffee grounds to make coffee and hair dryers to dry their hair. The majority of people may also think that the use of eggs, lemons, mustard, butter, and mayonnaise should be restricted to making delicious food in the kitchen. The Instructables.com community would disagree with this logic—they have discovered hundreds of inventive and surprising ways to use these and other common household materials to improve day-to-day life.

Did you know that tennis balls can protect your floors, fluff your laundry, and keep you from backing too far into (and thus destroying) your garage? How much do you know about aspirin? Sure, it may alleviate pain, but it can also be used to remove sweat stains, treat bug bites and stings, and prolong the life of your sputtering car battery. These are just a few of the quirky ideas that appear in *Unusual Uses for Ordinary Things*.

US $12.95 paperback ISBN: 978-1-62087-725-8

also available

Practical Duct Tape Projects

by Instructables.com, edited by Noah Weinstein

Duct tape has gotten a reputation as the quick-fix tape for every situation. However, did you know that you can use duct tape to create practical items for everyday use? Did you also know that duct tape now comes in a variety of colors, so your creations can be fun and stylish? Originating from Instructables, a popular project-based community made up of all sorts of characters with wacky hobbies and a desire to pass on their wisdom to others, *Practical Duct Tape Projects* contains ideas from a number of authors who nurse a healthy urge to create anything possible from duct tape.

Practical Duct Tape Projects provides step-by-step instructions on a variety of useful and fun objects involving duct tape. Guided through each endeavor by detailed photographs, the reader will create articles of clothing, tools, and more.

US $12.95 paperback ISBN: 978-1-62087-709-8

also available

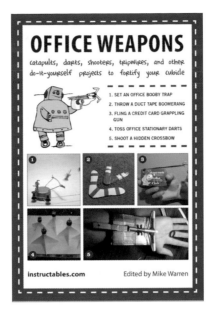

Office Weapons
Catapults, Darts, Shooters, Tripwires, and Other Do-It-Yourself Projects to Fortify Your Cubicle

by Instructables.com, edited by Mike Warren

Bored in your office? Did your coworker just prank you and you're wondering how to get him back? Is your boss constantly stealing your paperclips and you don't know how to keep his mitts away from your desk? *Office Weapons* gives you the complete step-by-step instructions for thirty different daring office pranks. Check out these simple but effective weapons fashioned from office materials and be prepared next time someone borrows your special stapler or leaves the copy machine jammed.

These projects are made by the best in the business; the office workers who actually need them! They say necessity is the mother of invention; leave it to the Instructables community to put that theory to the test!

US $14.95 paperback ISBN: 978-1-62087-708-1

also available

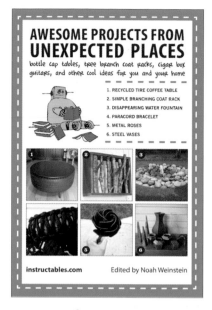

Awesome Projects from Unexpected Places
Bottle Cap Tables, Tree Branch Coat Racks, Cigar Box Guitars, and Other Cool Ideas for Your and Your Home
by Instructables.com, edited by Noah Weinstein

The term "crafting" used to call to mind woven baskets topped with bows, braided friendship bracelets, and painted angelic-faced figurines. Thanks to Instructables.com, crafting has shed its wings—and its ribbons—and has become a pastime appreciated by both men and women.

After reading *Awesome Projects from Unexpected Places*, readers will no longer panic when a coveted watchband breaks. Instead, they will coolly use a woven paracord to replace the band with little effort. When the living room needs a bit more life, crafters will rise to the occasion and deliver Dalí-inspired melting clocks, geometric cut-paper table lamps, and eco-friendly lights.

US $12.95 paperback ISBN: 978-1-62087-705-0

also available

Easy Vegetarian Recipes
Savory and Filling Dishes Featuring Healthy Veggies
by Instructables.com; edited by Sarah James

Originating from Instructables, a popular project-based community made up of all sorts of characters with wacky hobbies and a desire to pass on their wisdom to others, *Easy Vegetarian Recipes* is made up of recipes from a cast of cooks who demonstrate their culinary savvy and flavor combinations.

Easy Vegetarian Recipes gives full step-by-step instructions for creating delicious vegetarian dishes that even die-hard carnivores will crave. Written by cooks who can't get enough of veggies, each recipe contains pictures for an easy follow-along guide, even for those who spend little to no time in the kitchen.

The Instructables community offers a great mixture of tastes and cuisines. Italian, Mexican, American, and more will appease any picky eater as well as provide for those who are willing to try just about anything.

US $12.95 paperback ISBN: 978-1-62087-697-8